Instructor's Manual

WAYS TO WRITING

THIRD EDITION

Linda C. Stanley
Queensborough Community College

David Shimkin
Queensborough Community College

Allen H. Lanner
Queensborough Community College

MACMILLAN PUBLISHING COMPANY
New York

Macmillan Publishing Company is part of the
Maxwell Communications Group of Companies.

Printed in the United States of America

Macmillan Publishing Company
866 Third Avenue, New York, New York 10022

Maxwell Macmillan Canada, Inc.
1200 Eglinton Avenue East
Suite 200
Don Mills, Ontario M3C 3N1

Printing: 1 2 3 4 5 6 7   Year: 2 3 4 5 6 7 8

ISBN   0-02-415652-3

CONTENTS

WAYS TO WRITING--AN INTRODUCTION TO USING THE TEXT

Entering the Writing Classroom of the 1990's

The teacher who enters a writing classroom in the 1990's does so in a context dramatically different from that of even a decade ago. For those of us who began teaching composition before 1980, armed only with reader, handbook, and red pen, the surge of concern for teaching effective writing in the past decade is both hopeful and useful. For those of you who are teaching writing for the first time, you are entering a profession that has radically changed in recent years, perhaps even from when you sat in a freshman composition class yourself.

This metamorphosis of the teaching of writing can be attributed mainly to the profession's decision to both analyze the writing process and reintroduce classical rhetoric in order to teach a new generation of students less prepared than their forebears. Partly also the change can be attributed to the economic value that effective written expression has acquired in the workplace. Yet another reason is that the approach to the teaching of writing in today's college classrooms reflects the change over the last decade or so in the relationship between teacher and student.

It is almost certain that every reader of this manual has been affected in some way by the development of the student-centered classroom and collaborative learning. Thanks to the efforts of such members of the profession as Peter Elbow, Ken Macrorie, Donald Murray, Ken Bruffee and others, many teachers have cast off, or at least modified, their role as omniscient authority and become more of a co-learner and co-participant in the creative process.

Ways to Writing incorporates many of the classroom techniques associated with the writing process and collaborative learning, while at the same time offering ample materials for stressing both the new and old rhetoric. Rather than making an either/or choice between process-and product-centered modes of instruction, most instructors seem to use both methods, stressing the process of writing early in the semester, but focusing more intensely on classical methods of invention, arrangement, and style as the writing assignments demand greater organizational skills.

Approaching the Teaching of Writing Through a Series of Tasks

In each chapter of Ways to Writing, students are asked to complete a specific writing task or assignment. Each task is specific enough to give them a clear sense of what is required of them, yet flexible in that for subject matter it draws on their own interests, experiences, observation, and research.

Each task encourages students to see themselves in the role of inquirer--writers in active pursuit of a meaningful goal. While the subject matter of the tasks is familiar territory-- students' own experiences, places, and situations they know or can easily become acquainted with, media and issues that they are familiar with, and arguments and scientific inquiries of their own devising--yet they are asked to approach each task from a new angle so that a problem to be solved is the basic ingredient. Problems include seeking the surprising in their experiences, testing prejudices they hold, proving or disproving a hypothesis, evaluating the opinions of others through direct observation, explaining the effect of the media, and attempting to synthesize opposing arguments on an issue through critical thinking.

According to George Hillocks, in his <u>Research</u> <u>on</u> <u>Written</u> <u>Composition</u>: <u>New</u> <u>Directions</u> <u>for</u> <u>Teaching</u>, the task approach is "over two-and-a-half times more powerful than the traditional study of model pieces of writing" in improving quality of students' written texts. We have certainly found it to be so in our classrooms.

<u>Emphasizing</u> <u>the</u> <u>Dynamic</u> <u>and</u> <u>Cumulative</u> <u>Nature</u> <u>of</u> <u>the</u> <u>Tasks</u>

We hope that by becoming more aware of how they write, students will also learn more about themselves as writers: how they think, how they can learn more about a subject, how they can learn from their classmates about the process of writing, how they can address an audience. By taking them through a variety of tasks that make increasingly more difficult demands on their powers of invention and organization, we hope to make them conscious of their own writing growth. Because each task incorporates what the student has learned from the previous ones, the instructor can build on these already encountered writing strategies in subsequent assignments.

In developing <u>Ways</u> <u>to</u> <u>Writing</u>, we have tried to create a sequence of activities and suggestions that emphasize the dynamic nature of the tasks as they move from expressive to expository to persuasive to critical thinking. (For this aspect of the structure of the tasks, we are indebted to James Kinneavy for his four-part structure of expressive, referential--which he divides into exploratory and informative--persuasive, and literary writing--for which we have substituted literary analysis.)

Many instructors--and we have found this to be true across the curriculum--comment on their students' inadequacy in generalizing and reasoning critically, on the gap that separates their personal perceptiveness from some larger, more objective vision of things and events. We do not, however, imply such a split between subjective and objective, thought and feeling, idea and emotion. Students, in fact, tend to generalize all too freely, and every instructor can cite as evidence some weak, vaguely-written paragraph that tries to "cover" a subject like abortion or the plight of the homeless. What we have tried to accomplish is a series of tasks and strategies that enable students to become aware of how their general thinking can be directed more specifically to both subject and audience and their specific experiences inserted into a larger pattern.

Distinguishing Among the Aims of Writing

James Kinneavy, in his essay "The Basic Aims of Discourse" (see bibliography below), says that distinguishing between only two aims of writing--the expository and the creative--is "too simple." Along with many other theorists, he categorizes several aims, which he defines as the effect the writer has sought on the intended reader. These aims, of course, overlap.

Kinneavy distinguishes between external interpretation of the aims of a given piece of discourse, which is based on both writer and reader perceptions, and internal, which he believes is based on an analysis of the part of the communications triangle on which the writer focuses. When the writer emphasizes the writer, the aim is said to be expressive. When the focus is on the reader, the aim is persuasive. A concentration on the subject leads to referential discourse while a focus on the text itself indicates the creative aim. We have organized Ways to Writing according to these four aims: the expressive, which emphasizes the writer; the exploratory and the explanatory, which concentrate on the subject; the persuasive, which focuses on the reader; and the interpretive, which interprets the creative aim.

Expressive Aim. We begin with tasks that stress expressive writing. An expressive aim underlies many commonplace writing tasks--for example, a letter in which a student might describe her/his first impressions of college and recommend that a friend apply. Its familiarity is an asset early in the composition class, largely because students often will write more fluently and responsively about what they know.

Many students are terrified of the freshman composition class; they strain in the opening classes to learn what the teacher requires of them, in effect what dialect they must adopt in order to succeed in the course. Once the instructor assures them that it is their voice, however raw and undeveloped it may appear in their early writing, that the teacher and, more important, their fellow students find interesting, the more vital

their writing becomes. The journal thus becomes the safe haven in
which their voices can be tuned.

As they move through the tasks requiring a personal essay,
they gain confidence in their ability to say something that
matters to someone else, to describe an incident they have
observed or to explain their point of view on a subject. An
instructor will frequently find this stage of the term's work most
rewarding. It is often through this shared expression of personal
experiences that a class is drawn closer together into a cohesive,
cooperative union. Once this bond is established, the expository
and persuasive modes of writing that follow will be much less
intimidating.

An expressive aim, of course, is rarely absent from more
academic writing tasks. More often than not, when students are
called on to analyze reading material or draw inductive
conclusions about raw data, they are also expected to express
their point of view about the topic they are studying. The
lessons that expressive writing holds about clarifying one's point
of view for an audience whose perspective may be different remain
important as students engage in critical thinking and research.
The assignments in Part I are thus a useful foundation and point
of reference for later assignments in the text.

The Exploratory and Explanatory Aims. Kinneavy divides
referential writing into three categories: the exploratory, which
asks a question; the informative, which answers it; and the
scientific, which proves the answer. These subdivisions of the
referential aim in Ways to Writing correspond to the tasks in Part
II: Exploration; Part III: Explanation; and Part V: Writing About
Research, which, although scientific in content, we treat here as
having a more tentative aim, an exploratory aim, if you will.

Exploratory tasks are found in Chapters 4 and 5 of Ways to
Writing. These tasks call for students to investigate a place to
see if its good reputation is justified and to test a prejudgment
they have made. Assigning writing as a way of helping students
question and learn is becoming more and more frequent on college
campuses as instructors across the curriculum become involved in
the writing across the curriculum (writing-to-learn) movement.

Kinneavy believes each aim results in various genres, which
are distinguishable from the genres of other aims. In a recent
listing of exploratory genre (Conference on College Composition
and Communication 1990), he included (some) newspaper columns and
case studies. In Chapter 4, we ask the student to assume the role
of investigative reporter; and in Chapter 5, to write a case study
of the situation about which they have formed a prejudgment.
Other exploratory genres listed by Kinneavy include grant

proposals, progress reports, surveys, feasibility studies, some editorials.

Explanatory tasks are found in Chapters 6 and 7, in which we ask students to explain a family or cultural tradition or their perceptions of an aspect of the media. The assumption is that, in each task, students are answering a question the reader has asked, that students possess a storehouse of information that can be imparted to others. In his essay, Kinneavy lists news articles, reports, and summaries among his genres with an informative aim, and the essays produced for these tasks will contain elements of all three.

The Persuasive Aim. The current preoccupation with establishing a writer's socio-cultural origins--as in eurocentrism, phallocentrism and the like--reinforces the notion that no discourse is completely disinterested or value-free. All discourse, intentionally or not, is guided by a persuasive agenda. Whether or not one assents to the idea that the intentions of the writer are irrelevant to the actual discursive product, the emphasis on argumentative and persuasive techniques has given greater importance to the writer's own perception of the writing process.

Because the persuasive aim seems to subsume all the other writing aims, this creates an intense need to understand the cognitive functioning that results in arguments, directing them to specific audiences. This highlights the importance of studying critical thinking, the establishment and evaluation of evidence, the ways our daily negotiations with the world enjoin a rich repertoire of persuasive techniques. A discussion of argument as a writing aim can take us to the heart of the writing class as a place for examining how we create discourse, how we can foster a dialogical relation with our audience, how we can participate fully in a community of writers.

The Interpretive Aim. The act of interpretation brings into play all of the other writing aims in its devotion to the fullest possible interplay of writer, reader, and text. The writer expresses a personal connection to the text, seeing in it an imaginative rendering of the human situation, a resonance of the reader's own expressive needs.

In writing about literature, the reader explores the world of the text and in the process defamiliarizes a comfortable engagement with her or his own world of received ideas, opinions, and habits. To interpret, therefore, is to open up a new possibility for conceiving and defining the self. It is also, in more traditional terms, to argue a position based on evidence drawn from the text, evidence broadly defined in part as figurative structures, narrative devices, and cultural and psychological insights.

Working With the Stages of the Writing Process

As we developed the organization of the text, we tried to consider the stages of the writing process as they occur in the completion of a writing task: analysis of purpose, task, audience, generation of ideas, writing and revising. We recognize, of course, that the writing process is much messier than this--is recursive, if you will--and we correspondingly refer backwards and forwards as we move through each chapter as a way of demonstrating for students the essentially chaotic, spontaneous series of acts of which the writing process is composed.

The deliberately repetitive organization of these strategies from chapter to chapter, however, frees students from the frustration and confusion that they often encounter when given an assignment requiring problem solving: students working on an expository task in the later chapters of the text can apply the same interpretative and pragmatic sequence of strategies to that task as they have to earlier ones. Strategies can also be interchanged among chapters as students acquire a repertory of methods of invention and audience analysis and of arrangement patterns.

For each stage of the writing process there are exercises that can be used as written or as modified by the instructor. We have tried to provide ample and varied class activities that we hope are useful and even at times entertaining.

Focusing on the Noteworthy Features of Each Chapter Section

Purpose. Our intent in this section is to offer a clear sense of both the practical applications that might be made of a chapter's task and the particular writing skills that it helps students develop. Students often have legitimate questions about what purposes a writing assignment serves. The purpose sections offer twofold answers--explaining the everyday uses to which expressive, exploratory, explanatory, and persuasive writing may be put as well as the pedagogical rationale behind a given task, so that students can place it as part of the progression from one aim of writing to another.

Task. The task section announces the task and offers some suggestions for approaching it in terms of audience, subject, and arrangement. It highlights how the material in the sections that follow will help students move through the process of writing the essay assigned in each chapter. Students are made aware from the start of how the lessons on generating ideas or audience in each chapter are relevant to the specific task at hand.

In selecting tasks, our intention is to provide students with a purposeful but interesting writing topic. It is not enough just to assign a topic drawn from students' own experience. They have to feel the topic will create something worth sharing with others and that they themselves can learn from the experience of writing about it. Instructors who prefer to choose topics of their own will find that our tasks are quite flexible, adapting to most of the commonly assigned topics in college writing programs.

Our tasks require students to examine their experiences and observations from a changed perspective: to see their actions over a period of time; to observe a place during a visit or over a number of visits; to explain the significance of a custom or ritual. Because they generate questions and problems, the tasks also generate class discussion and activities, particularly within peer groups where students can exchange strategies for completing each task.

Because the tasks progress in difficulty, we do not suggest that the instructor vary the order of tasks to any great degree. While the research paper may be introduced earlier in the semester so that students can begin the stages of this work, persuasive writing, for example, with its demanding reasoning and marshalling of evidence, is best kept until later in the course, and expressive writing seems to us to be a logical starting point. Some instructors may, however, prefer to assign the task for Chapter 2 late in the term, after students have written a substantial portion of their journal: while this task is a valuable introduction to the skill of generalization, it also offers students the opportunity to assess their development as writers and thinkers over the entire course of the semester.

Writing the Essay. The advantages of taking students through the writing process, showing them how they can incorporate their prewriting activities into the actual writing of an essay, should be obvious. In each chapter, we introduce a different method of generating ideas, addressing the needs of an audience, and arranging an essay that students may find useful in a variety of rhetorical contexts; we then direct the students' attention to how these methods will help them accomplish the specific chapter's task.

Generating Ideas. We expect that this part of each chapter will create a great deal of class discussion by offering students some specific, practical suggestions for invention. Each chapter employs a different heuristic for its task. In Chapters 1 and 2, for example, we establish the journal as a critical tool for self-analysis as well as a technique that can be used for writing assignments including but not limited to personal essays. We include as early as Chapter 2 and as late as Chapter 11 cross-references to and descriptions of the techniques of brainstorming and clustering that we introduce in detail in Chapter 6, in order to encourage students to see the relevance of such techniques in a variety of writing situations. We do not expect this chapter section to function as mere information, however; each section presents a method of invention that we feel works best with the chapter task. And as each task requires more complex inventive strategies from the writer, so does the heuristic demand a greater degree of comprehension. The exercises here--as in other sections of each chapter--are to be used selectively. We do not expect the instructor to use them all; those that apply directly to the chapter task will invariably prove most useful.

We have tried to effect a workable combination of traditional rhetoric with the most recent approaches to heuristic techniques. Classical invention strategies are discussed in the section on the Classical Questions in Chapters 5 - 10, induction in Chapters 8 and 10, and deduction in Chapter 8. The Explorer's Questions of Chapter 4, which use the "tagmemic heuristic" as the inventive device, are borrowed from linguistics; the journalist's questions of Chapter 3 are borrowed from journalism and rhetoric (Kenneth Burke's pentad); and freewriting (Chapter 1) comes ultimately from psycholinguistics.

Audience. The tasks for each chapter of our text place a good deal of emphasis on the student's awareness of an audience other than the teacher for his/her writing. We do not exclude the teacher as the ultimate judge of each essay's interest and effectiveness, for of course he or she must still be responsible for the student's grade. But the extravagant ruses that students were often unwittingly forced into because of the need to "give the teacher what she wants" (although an awareness of audience in itself) are no longer necessary. In our approach, students become conscious of several audiences--themselves in both private and public roles, their teacher and classmates, and the real or imagined world of selected other writers and readers.

In Ways to Writing, students begin with the need to hear themselves, to be conscious of their own individual voice--as much as this can be determined--and then move to express the other voices they may assume in their daily life for other audiences. With the change in aim from expressive to expository, students' awareness of audience expands to take into account the lay reader, more informed readers, the academic community. In writing persuasively, students create a dramatic situation, a case, in which they must directly confront people whose lives will in some way be affected by their argument.

We discuss these audience situations in the abstract but also make them an integral part of the completion of each task. The variety of tasks places students in a number of roles vis-a-vis their audience. The decisions that writing for an audience requires can form the basis of lively class discussion of each writing assignment. Students particularly enjoy playing with the idea of different roles and audience contexts. The exercises encourage them to use their knowledge of print and other media where audience assumes an obviously important role in the nature of the message.

Arranging Your Essay. Students can apply directly and purposively all their previous thinking about audience and invention to the problems of arrangement that only arise as one actually writes. Their decisions about audience (suggested in the Audience Analysis Guide) relate directly to the task at hand. The stages the student writing the model essay went through recapitulate the process of other students as well. In addition, professional essays are provided to show student writers how other authors have confronted similar writing tasks.

Students will most likely have many questions about the steps outlined for each task. Peer group meetings on specific writing problems can be very helpful in getting students over some of the initial hurdles of approaching their task. For example, in Chapter 4, students can prepare interview questions for their visit to a place or decide how they would prefer a place unfamiliar to them to be described.

Focus on Form and Style. Formal and stylistic elements are introduced in this section first in general terms applicable to any writing task, then in specific terms directed to the task at hand. We encourage instructors to familiarize themselves with these sections and then to take up in class what seems pertinent as it arises. The formalities of developing a thesis, of writing an introduction and a conclusion, of establishing unity and coherence within and between paragraphs are the focus of early chapters both because of the tasks students face in these chapters and because these are often matters taken up early in the writing class. But an instructor might want to skip ahead, for example, to the section on sentence combining in Chapter 5, to illustrate some sentence problems early in the term. Our intention is not to be encyclopedic but to provide a manageable and useful introduction to structural and stylistic problems that arise in class discussions and workshop sessions.

Rewriting. We find it essential that students receive some feedback on their own writing. To facilitate this response, we provide students with an Audience Response Guide where they can register some thoughts about papers they have heard or read in peer groups. The instructor can reproduce the guide to hand out or students can write their comments directly on the writer's draft. This section also includes a peer review of the student rough draft prepared in the Writing the Essay section as well as a "final" draft in response.

Each chapter undertakes a different revising and editing problem. Students are frequently overwhelmed by the sea of red that overflows the traditionally-graded paper. Therefore, we introduce revising strategies gradually and cumulatively. By focusing on specific, limited revising decisions, students become more confident in their ability to accomplish each task and grow in their openness to others' writing efforts.

A <u>Checklist</u> of <u>Questions</u> to <u>Consider.</u> New to this edition, this Checklist summarizes for students through a series of questions the main features of the chapter's task. While we have placed the Checklist after the Audience Response Guide, in the assumption that the student's "other self" will take over after the peer critiquing process and be the final arbiter of the revisions needed, you may want students to refer to the Checklist questions while writing their rough drafts as well.

The Checklist also provides you, as the instructor, with a list of the primary traits required by the task for use in evaluating students' essays.

<u>Becoming</u> <u>Aware</u> of <u>Yourself</u> <u>as</u> <u>a</u> <u>Writer</u>. These questions ask student writers to think about their own writing process and to respond critically to questions raised during the chapter. We do not intend them to be used as test questions and specifically encourage students to use them as journal topics. They may also be used as possible subjects for short, in-class writing exercises, class discussion, or student/teacher conference.

Chapter Notes

INTRODUCTION: WAYS TO WRITING

New to this edition, this chapter introduces students to the
concept of writing as a process, a process that engages the
writer's psyche as well as his or her rhetorical skills. As
Scott, one of our students, moves through a process in the writing
of an essay we had requested, he records in his journal his
decisions and indecisions along the way. From his agony in
procrastinating to the choices he makes about topic, content, and
manner of writing, other student writers may recognize, if not
precisely their own process, then certainly the trials and errors,
the starts and stops of the activity of writing.

In the context of Scott's recording of his efforts in his
journal, we also introduce the flow of each chapter, the headings
and subheadings of the text as they present students with the
decisions that they must make in pursuing the completion of the
chapter's writing task.

To encourage students to think of themselves as writers, we
stress the relative autonomy of the decision-making process any
writer must move through. The choices, we tell them, are theirs,
and the finished product will reflect the paths they choose to
follow, the roads they themselves decide to travel. A textbook,
indeed a writing course, can only alert them to the junctures at
which choices must be made, give them a context for making them,
indicate the consequences, and hope for the best.

In teaching the Introduction, if students have not yet read
it, you may want to begin with Frost's poem, which is printed only
in part here as we assume student familiarity with it, and then
ask students to list and discuss the choices they think Scott made
in writing his final draft. A subsequent comparison with his
rough draft may lead them to revise their list and enlarge their
discussion of his process of revision. If students have already
read the entire Introduction, they can form their list from both
drafts and from his journal.

Reading Scott's journal account can serve several pedagogical
aims: First, it can introduce the idea of writing as a process.
Despite the widespread acceptance of the process approach to
teaching writing, many writing teachers do not utilize it, and
therefore students may be largely unfamiliar with it.

Second, reading Scott's journal can introduce students to keeping a journal; although the journal is widely assigned, some students may never have kept one. For those who have kept a personal journal, keeping what Peter Elbow calls a process journal about one's writing may present a new subject matter.

Finally, and perhaps most important at this juncture, you may want to ask your students to write a journal entry in which they describe their own writing process, perhaps comparing it to Scott's. While students may not think they have a process, being asked to describe it may encourage them to crystallize what they do when they write. Asking students to share their journal entries and discuss how each other writes will prepare students to be aware both of their successes in completing a piece of writing and of those stages which impede their progress. Knowing that others find writing both pleasurable and difficult will encourage them to begin the course with anticipation.

CHAPTER ONE: WRITING ABOUT YOURSELF--KEEPING A JOURNAL

Ways to Writing begins by asking students to experiment with expressive writing by keeping a daily journal. We have found that it is a good idea to give students an opportunity to write freely about themselves, without having to worry at first over how their work will be judged. One rationale for the first chapter's focus on journal writing is simply to loosen students up, to give them a chance to relax with and enjoy the act of writing.

At the same time, the self-expressive emphasis in Chapter 1, as well as in the following two chapters, is presented to introduce students to some of the primary elements of the writing process. (See the comments on Expressive Aims in the section Ways To Writing-Introduction above.) To complete the task for Chapter 1, students are encouraged to generalize about the patterns of thought and feeling that emerge in their journal.

The act of journal keeping thus becomes the first in a series of lessons throughout the text about the importance of developing generalizations out of specifics and of using concrete details to illustrate generalized concepts. Students learn that it also can be a heuristic, a way of developing material for a formal essay.

One further reason for the stress on expressive writing is worth noting here. By keeping a daily journal, students are given an opportunity to test out the voice in which they write most naturally, what we call their "private voice." They do not have to try to sound "intelligent" for their teacher or "cool" for their peers, at least as long as their journal entries remain private. By learning about how they can best express themselves to themselves, they may begin to develop a better sense of their personal style and point of view, a sense that we feel is important to have as a basis upon which to make adjustments in one's writing when one writes for others.

What follows are more specific comments on the noteworthy features of each of the four sections in Chapter 1. Included are suggestions about how you might teach each section and comments on the exercises in those sections where they appear.

Purpose

Students may have a lot of initial questions about the purposes of both expressive writing in general and keeping a journal in particular. Discussing the ways in which self-expression can serve public as well as private aims is a useful means of introducing students to the hows and whys of journal writing. You should clarify at the start the degree to which you expect your students to focus on their personal life and experiences, the degree to which they are to focus on field research, reading material or other sources of information. (See the section below on The Journal in Ways to Teaching-Suggested Strategies.) In either case, you will want to encourage students to be as open and honest as possible when they write in their journal. Some discussion of how private this writing will be (whether you will ask to look at the journal or at edited selections from it) may help at the start.

Task: Writing a Journal

In addition to discussing the purposes and subject matter of the journal, it is a good idea when assigning this task to devote some time to the routine and format the class will follow in keeping their journals. When and how often should they write in the journal? Do you suggest they try a double-entry method, writing at first only on left-hand pages (or the left-hand columns of divided pages), then filling in the blank right-hand space with reaction to, comment on, analysis of their left-hand entries? Will you encourage them to use the journal as a heuristic for subsequent tasks? How, if at all, will the journal be evaluated?

Writing the Journal

Generating Ideas: Free Writing. Free Writing exercises are an effective way of getting students started on their journals. You should keep in mind, however that while students are delighted with the idea of free writing, with all its anti-English class establishment connotations, it is very rare that they produce writing that is really free. As the examples in this section show, their writing does not very much resemble the stream of consciousness examples found in Joyce, Faulkner, or the Surrealists. In fact, their free writing in many ways resembles the writing we find in their "polished" drafts. To write truly freely requires a lot of practice and more consciousness than most students possess of their own thoughts, even, as the Surrealists' experience revealed, more consciousness than most artists possess naturally, unaided by extra stimulation.

This is not to say that because students still tend to segment their thinking with punctuation and paragraphs, free writing is of no value to them. By relaxing as they write, they still generate more ideas on a subject than they might ordinarily. Since free writing cannot be criticized, the role of the instructor is to encourage students in as many ways as possible to open up, to overcome inhibitions or even writer's block, and to produce as great a volume of writing as they can on a subject.

Since students, like the rest of us, tend to think in patterns, one way to encourage greater freedom in writing is to

14

have them read their free writings to each other. For example, in writing about a lemon, Writer 1 drew on her present associations with lemons, while Writer 2 drew on an early memory. By hearing the other's approach, both might expand their repertory of ways in which such an object might be approached. In Exercise 2, the student has written a very abstract piece on a pen and its uses. Hearing another's piece filled with physical detail might suggest to the writer another direction in which to go.

We have found a lemon to be one of the most evocative objects to free write about. In Exercise 1 students may discover items that have one particularly sensuous association for them, such as the touch of an old pair of jeans, the sight of a painting, the sound of a car motor, the taste of spaghetti. In trying to locate an object that has multi-sensual associations, like a lemon, students may think of, for example, a rose, an old baseball glove, a piece of wet bark, a squeaking door, or an onion.

The reflective impulse of the free writing on Hallowe'en /Aggie makes an interesting comparison with the narrative tendency of the following passage about the nightmarish trip. As the former writer charmingly - and authentically--makes clear, she is quite ambivalent about the "advantages of being an adult." Her claims to these advantages notwithstanding, one senses that she would like to experience Hallowe'en as a child once again and that she regrets the difficult times she and Aggie, particularly Aggie, have had in going through their rites of passage. In the right-hand entry of a double-entry journal, she might develop her thoughts about this basic ambivalence.

Should "a holiday you went on" not prove worth mining for some students in fulfilling Exercise 3, then you might suggest "first day on a first job" or a "party in your honor." We have suggested that students not think "too hard" about a subject of study in Exercise 4 before beginning to free write in order to head off a sense that they are taking a test, which they usually are doing when writing on such a subject. They should instead be encouraged to explore their own feelings about the subject as well as what they may recall about it; this approach helps them avoid writer's block and may provide the student with a unique angle from which to approach the subject in subsequent writing about it.

The question that we ask at the end of Exercise 4 prepares the way for students to begin seeking patterns in their journal. For some initial practice with this, students might try Peter Elbow's two-hour free-writing heuristic in which they are asked to stop after 45 minutes and evaluate ("sum up the pattern that emerges") what they have written and then start off again in a new direction by writing about the summary. Elbow's method encourages students to seek the generalization behind their experiences. If students cannot locate a pattern to generalize about in their first free writing, you might give them a series of prompts based on the Classical Questions listed in Ch. 5 ("what can it be compared to?" "what caused it?" "what effect did it have?" etc.) and ask them which question(s) they seem to be asking and answering.

Note that the examples in this section come from the journals of both students and professional writers. Some class discussion of the different voices a reader hears moving from one example to another may prove helpful in preparing students for the audience section on voice that follows.

The exercises in Some Practice in Starting Your Journal can, of course, utilize free writing. At the same time, students who prefer taking a more structured approach to journal writing should be encouraged to do so.

Another way of getting students started tracing patterns in their journal is to assign one or more of the suggested topics in Some Practice in Using Your Journal or topics of your own devising. This set of exercises asking the students to experiment with their journal entries cannot be assigned, however, until students have been writing in their journal for at least a week. We suggest that the class move on to the audience section, before any of the experiments with journal entries are assigned.

(Note that if you prefer to deemphasize the expressive element in your students' writing and start your students immediately on more expository work, you may still assign Chapter 1. The journal is a valid heuristic, no matter what the writer's dominant purpose. Also, you may want to assign the sections on Private Voice in conjunction with either the Audience sections of Chapters 2 and 3 or the Focus sections on style of Chapters 6 and 7.)

Addressing Your Audience: Private Voice. Students often express conflicting opinions about which of the notes to Professor Ames sounds the most "honest" or might be the most effective. A discussion of this matter is a good way of introducing the concept of a voice. This concept then may be clarified by some discussion of Ken Macrorie's ideas about "truthful" writing, introduced in the sub-section on Discovering Your Own Voice. The importance of looking for unexpected perceptions and of using language that is as concise and yet as detailed as possible is developed in the following material written by a student who was mugged. The exercises that follow on Some Practice with Voice illustrate in a variety of ways that there are differences in voice just as there are differences in character (exercises 2, 3, 4, 5) and that the words we choose to express ourselves can either convey or mask what is distinctive about our character (exercises 1, 5, 6, 7, 8, 9).

The sub-section on the writer's point of view introduces material that is developed in the audience sections of Chapters 2 and 3.

For the second exercise in Some Practice with Your Point of View, you might want to substitute another brief narrative in order to elicit a variety of points of view. In this example, the audience might respond in a number of ways to the late performers.

Becoming Aware of Yourself as a Writer

We suggest that you have students respond to these questions by writing in their journals. Peer group or class discussion can then follow. Question 1 asks students to assess how they feel about writing now that they have kept a journal. Questions 2-5 focus on the relationship between journal writing, the writer, other acts of writing, and the writer's possible audience. Questions 6 and 7 ask students to assess the lessons in Chapter 1 on voice and point of view. Discussion of these questions can serve as a good introduction to Chapters 2 and 3.

CHAPTER TWO: WRITING ABOUT YOURSELF--EXPRESSING YOUR POINT OF VIEW

In Chapter 2, students write an essay expressing the point of view that emerges toward a subject from a series of related entries in their journal. Because they are asked to use the private voice of their journal to develop a piece of public writing, Chapter 2 offers a good opportunity to discuss the role that audience plays in an act of writing, to begin examining the relationships between a writer, a subject, and a reader. Although students write for a reader who is sympathetic to their point of view in this assignment, they still will feel pressure to focus on an appropriate subject for others to read about and introduce that subject in a way that sparks a reader's interest.

The challenge introduced in Chapter 1 of generalizing about a pattern of journal entries is developed at length in Chapter 2 as students work to shape their subject into a thesis statement.

Although a student may write about a personal subject in response to the task for Chapter 2, this is not necessarily the case. Much will depend on the kind of entries--on the range of subject matter--that you have suggested for the journal. We have included, in fact, a student essay in which the writer has chosen to express her point of view on Theoreau, passages of whose journals are included in Chapter 2 along with excerpts of a chapter of <u>Walden</u> that is in part structured out of them.

Purpose

It may be worthwhile to discuss the kinds of journal entries students might want others to read. What might readers get out of such entries? Would certain entries--or an essay about them-- primarily appeal or be of interest to readers whose frame of reference or point of view is similar to the writer's?

One way of initiating such a class discussion is by first having the students form peer groups (see the section on "Arranging Your Essay" below) in which they share and comment on one another's entries as possible subjects for an essay.

Task: <u>Writing</u> <u>an</u> <u>Essay</u> <u>Based</u> <u>on</u> <u>Your</u> <u>Journal</u>

The task that we have structured for the first essay emphasizes writing about patterns of thought and interest that emerge as a student keeps a journal. The idea that this discovery may surprise the student can be interpreted to mean simply "impress" or "interest." We have used "surprise" in order to direct attention to the conflict between the expected and the unexpected in one's experience since such a sense of conflict often provides valuable perceptions.

Because the task may lead some students to write about highly personal topics, this possibility should be discussed in class and ground rules laid. If you choose to let students write about any self-discovery they make in their journals, they may prefer to keep what they write as private as possible. If this is the case, peer group work (see Revising section below) may not be introduced until Chapter 3. Or you may suggest that students only write about discoveries they are willing to share with others.

Writing Your Essay

Generating Ideas: Tracing a Pattern in Your Journal. Note that although we do not introduce the activity of working with a peer group until later in this chapter (see "Arranging Your Essay" below), you may want to have students work together on tracing a pattern in the series of journal entries by Margaret Ryan.

The exercises at the end of the Generating Ideas section asking students to experiment with their journal entries may be usefully introduced at this point. These exercises engage the students in a review of their journal entries with an eye to generalizing about what self-discoveries they can make. Assigning one or more of these exercises is a good way of introducing the notion of a shaping idea or thesis, (See sections on Arranging Your Essay and Focus on Form below). Such an assignment also may initiate a discussion of how an essay might be arranged by moving back and forth between students' generalizations about themselves and the concrete details in their journal entries that prompted them to formulate their generalizations.

Addressing Your Audience: The Sympathetic Reader. Focusing attention on the student's journal entries about her sociology class is one way of beginning a class discussion of the kind of material with which a journal writer might go public. The two sets of exercises following these entries should help students, first, to clarify the concept of point of view, and second, to select an emerging point of view from their own journal that might prove a legitimate subject for an essay.

Arranging Your Essay. It is worth noting that this section and the following on Writing Your Rough Draft each includes an example of selections from journals that form the material of essays, one by Henry David Thoreau, the other by a student. The rough draft of the student's essay is included in Writing Your Rough Draft, while the revised draft is included in the section on Rewriting.

Students are also introduced to peer group work as a collaborative learning strategy in this section. By working in groups, students can test out their reactions to the journal entries and essay by Thoreau. Brainstorming allows for group support in the difficult process of puzzling out what point of view emerges from Thoreau's journal and how it is reflected in the shaping idea of "Where I Lived, and What I Lived For."

Class discussion of Thoreau and of the shaping idea students are developing for the first essay assignment follows well from this group work.

Writing Your Rough Draft. Tracing the changes made by the student from journal entries to rough draft to final draft is a good way of reinforcing Chapter One's lessons on how we do make adjustments in our private voice when we write for others and of introducing the first lessons on revising strategies. Also, noting what details in the original journal entries might have prompted the student to generalize as she did about herself is another way of introducing students to or strengthening their understanding of the concept of a shaping idea.

Note that at the end of this section, we open discussion of where and when students will work on their essays. (Matters of presentation are taken up in the section on Revising below.)

Focus on Form: Stating a Thesis/Writing an Introduction

Students may want to spend some time discussing academic conventions. Often they enter a writing class with the notion that there is a right and a wrong way to write for a teacher. The idea that conventions of form (and style) are less rigid but also broader in their applications than students might imagine can be liberating for many students, who respond well to the comparison between informal and formal conventions.

The section on stating a thesis offers a class the opportunity to talk about the writing process as students examine the train of thought that the writer of "Henry David Thoreau" followed to her main point.

It is worth stressing that an introduction is often written last. But it is also important to emphasize the individuality of the writing process. While some students may choose to adopt the method that the writer of "Henry David Thoreau" used to develop a thesis statement, others should be encouraged to experiment with their own ways of formulating a thesis and incorporating it into an introduction.

Rewriting

The idea of a peer group offering a critical reading of the rough draft of each student's essay is introduced here (see the section above on Setting Up Peer Groups). If you choose to wait until Chapter 3 to begin peer group work, because of the possibility that some students will respond to the task for Chapter 2 by writing a highly personal essay, you may serve as the reader of the rough draft; or, you may encourage students to answer the Audience Response Guide questions about their own drafts from the perspective of the "other self."

The process of revision can be introduced here by having a class review the peer group critique of the student essay along with the revision made in response to this critique. Discussing why the student decided to revise her introduction and her conclusion should help students revise their own rough draft with an eye to unifying the essay around a clearly expressed shaping idea. And pointing out instances where she made her language more concise or more detailed may be of help to students who are working to develop as honest a voice as possible in their revised essay. A clearly expressed shaping idea and an honest voice can then become two major criteria upon which the grade for the essay is determined.

Note that the mechanics of presenting a final draft are touched upon here. You may want to amend the material on Presentation to suit your own requirements.

Becoming Aware of Yourself as a Writer

The questions here can be a guide to find out what difficulties students encountered in fulfilling this task. You might want to collect their journals at this point to see what problems have arisen either in their group discussions or their writing activities and/or to use their responses to these questions as openers for student conferences. Because students are often intimidated at the thought of having their writing examined so closely, the questions we pose are intended to be exploratory and not the basis for establishing their grades.

CHAPTER THREE: WRITING ABOUT AN INCIDENT--REPORTING AN EXPERIENCE

In this chapter we turn to the daily newspaper in order to show how important facts are to the writer, and how important a role the audience plays in the selection and presentation of those facts. The journalist's questions are a very simple, even obvious starting point for a discussion of how the writer gathers material and then submits it in finished form for an audience. For students writing an expressive paper at the beginning of their writing course, this emphasis on the accumulation of concrete detail is quite helpful. It generates material for them and helps them to focus on the essential elements of the task.

The task for this chapter is to write on a personal experience, but we ask students to do so in light of their audience's frame of reference and point of view. This awareness of audience makes the distinction between expressive and expository less important than the need to adapt to the specific roles of writer and reader. Once students learn to recognize the importance of the writer's relationship to an audience, their whole perception of the writing process begins to take shape.

We usually spend considerable time at the beginning of the semester examining the nature of this relationship. We set up peer groups and ask students to interview each other to determine their frames of reference and point of view. Not only does this enable them to know each other better, but they learn how diverse an audience can be in its interests and experiences. More important, it sends them back to their own writing with an eye for what details and observations will work for them. The Eiseley and Angelou essays are vivid narratives that offer insight into the writers' selection of detail and their awareness of their audience. You can also try this inquiry into a writer's detail with local newspapers or nationally published magazines.

Because an important role in this chapter is played by narrative, you may want to investigate this even further in class. We sometimes ask students to narrate the story of their getting to class that period. It becomes clearer after several students relate their experience that even the most mundane account is the result of very careful, if unconscious, selection of detail arranged into a precise pattern of narrative. We then discuss how this pattern might be altered to serve a particular purpose of both writer and audience. Some students relate a predictable order of actions, such as "I shut off the alarm, washed up, had breakfast, walked the dog, took the No. 14 bus to school, got to the campus and went to this class." Others focus more specifically on details, such as an unusual looking person on the bus, a near accident on the road, an unexpected meeting with a personal friend. By focusing on specificity, we begin to uncover more and more layers of "fact" and how the journalist's questions can lead to many interesting personal accounts. But as this chapter shows, facts don't exist in a vacuum; they are a creation, so to speak, of a specific observer for a specific audience.

We realize that many instructors like to begin with more expository assignments and exercises in arrangement and rhetorical strategy. This can be done quite easily through the journalist's questions, and, in fact, many of the activities and exercises in this chapter work just as well with expository assignments. The focus sections on formulating and introducing a shaping idea in Chapter 2 and on paragraph structure and making transitions in this chapter work efficiently with writing tasks geared to a current-traditional rhetorical methodology.

Purpose

You might want to introduce this chapter by having the class write for 10 or 15 minutes on some incident that occurred that day or the day before. After breaking into small groups, the students can read their narratives to each other, looking for concrete details that make an event stand out. Students can quickly come to some conclusions about the relative effectiveness of the papers they hear. Without stressing the ranking of papers they have heard, you can ask them to pinpoint those details that a reader might find memorable.

Another way of introducing the role of the audience is to duplicate versions of a recent event as reported by a local newspaper and news magazine like Time. Students will often be quite observant, and indeed critical, about the embellishment of "fact." This can lead into the whole problem of distinguishing the objective from the subjective in autobiographical narrative. This distinction can readily be highlighted when students interview each other and write short biographies based on the information provided by the interviewee.

Task: Writing About an Incident

We spend a considerable amount of time with our classes discussing just what we mean by an incident that changed their thoughts or caused them to reassess their feelings. Clearly, this is not an assignment in which they can reach for breezy narratives that to most readers will be clichéd and unrevealing, such as "My Vacation in Acapulco" or "My Driving Test." We usually ask our students to reflect more deeply into what events have affected them without necessarily prying into their personal secrets. We ask them to imagine a reader responding with the question "So what?" to their choice of incident. In group work, they can submit their topics to other students and get some response to

their intended narrative. The Eiseley essay can be used here as
an example of a meaningful narrative, one that doesn't seem to
tell a crucial story but on reflection tells us much about the
writer and his relation to his personal life, his work, and his
home. We stress to our students that it is in the seemingly small
incidents in our lives that we often express ourselves most fully;
the Angelou essay offers a telling example.

Writing Your Essay

Generating Ideas: The Journalist's Questions. The
distinction made here between the journalist and the essayist is
of course a tentative one. Certainly Talese does more than "tell"
what happened at Cocoa Beach as John Glenn went into orbit. You
might want to examine with your class the different methods of
selecting details that the author has used. The economical
description, the use of quotation, the restrained drama--these
stylistic decisions can also be discussed as you go further into
the writer`s frame of reference and point of view in the Audience
section of this chapter.

Because student expressive writing often contains factual
gaps that puzzle the reader, the journalist's questions provide a
handy and practical tool. Realizing that they have to address
their audience in very specific ways, they will be less likely to
assume knowledge that the reader simply cannot have. We find the
questions a useful means of getting students to concretize the
difference between "showing" and "telling." By holding students
accountable to the reader early on in their writing, you can move
into other more complex matters in subsequent tasks.

Another interesting exercise is to have students list and
then discuss different motives for narrative, different purposes
that telling a story can serve.

Note we have found this an appropriate task for introducing
students to the double-entry notebook. The exercise of using the
journal as a double-entry notebook in itself illustrates how
expressive writing can be turned to public purposes. At the same
time, it gets students started on generating ideas for their essay
for Chapter 3.

Also, while many students will search their memory in order
to find a subject and select details for this task, you might
introduce the usefulness of field research at this point.

Addressing Your Audience: The "Intended" Reader(s). We have
focused this section on the students' perception of their
classmates. We ask the class to begin with an analysis of a
classmate's frame of reference and point of view. Depending

on the relative hetero- or homogeneity of your own students, you might wish to pursue with students some subject that reveals the important role of the reader's background and attitude.

For additional practice with point of view, you might "stage" an incident in class to elicit varied responses to what actually happened. One of our colleagues faked a loud argument with another student, and the differing versions of this prearranged theater provided a vivid model of the role that frame of reference and point of view play in the analysis of an event.

The exercises in the reader's frame of reference and point of view are intended for work with peer groups. Students can quite readily come up with some conclusions about the frame of reference of their group through brief interviews. Writing brief biographies and then reading them in class can be an effective introduction to the chapter task that follows.

The second exercise in Some Practice with A Reader's Point of View offers an example of the importance that the writer's choice of words has in determining point of view. You might want to spend some time analyzing the different voices and their possible identities. Students should be able to recognize the "types" that emerge from these voices. The exercises on inference offer further practice in drawing generalizations out of specific data. They also may be useful in initiating discussions of the ambiguous and relative nature of any audience analysis, as may the exercises on making inferences about an audience.

Students should be encouraged to work with the Audience Analysis Guide as one means of determining the criteria for selecting and ordering the details of their narrative.

Arranging Your Essay: The Shaping Idea, Narration and Exposition. Before your students write their essays, you might want to analyze with them Eiseley's, Angelou's, and the student writer's relationship to their audience and what they expect a reader to perceive through their use of details. Students may puzzle, for example, over Eiseley's ability to determine his dog's thoughts and may want to know how this can be allowed in a factual narrative. They may also want to know what leeway they can take with the facts of their own narratives. We discourage students who want to be "creative" with the events of their lives, asking them to refer to their journals if they feel in need of material to write about.

<u>Focus</u> <u>on</u> <u>Form</u>: <u>Paragraph</u> <u>Structure/Making</u> <u>Transitions</u>

<u>Paragraph</u> <u>Structure</u>. While it has become fashionable in some circles to disparage the traditional method of teaching paragraph structure--or the teaching of paragraphs at all-- particularly since professional writers often seem to follow no logic in constructing their own but adhere instead to some organic principle, we have taken the position that student writers--and perhaps professional writers as well - would do better to carefully structure their paragraphs. We have tried to be reasonable by recognizing that the topic sentence need not appear at the outset, but we stress that it does need to appear somewhere in the paragraph and with a rationale for its placement (see Exercise 4). Since Marya Mannes's paragraph does not contain a topic sentence, students might discuss whether or not including one, perhaps the one we supply, would improve the reader's comprehension of her meaning.

In Paragraph a of Exercise 1 the student writer actually began with sentence #2. The conclusion (Exercise 3) restates the point more specifically.

The student writer's actual topic sentence in Paragraph b was sentence #2. The paragraph has no conclusion as such although the last sentence ends on a dramatic and therefore effective note.

Paragraph c originally began with sentence #2 (second sentence). It has no conclusion, depending instead on its narrative development to create a sense of closure.

The original topic sentence for Paragraph a of Exercise 2 was "I became an avid skier that first day." Paragraph b originally began "I felt anxious while the plane climbed and then leveled out." Paragraph c was introduced with the sentence "It seemed like one more of our typical trips to the beach."

<u>Making</u> <u>Transitions</u>. The focus on transitions occurs at this point in the text because of 1) its importance for writing and understanding narrative and 2) the sense of order and coherence of arrangement it encourages in student writers. Most of the examples we use in the exercises are narrative paragraphs. You might wish to combine this Focus section with the one on sentence combining in Chapter 5.

After students have written rough drafts and formed peer groups in which to read their essays, you can emphasize the importance of transitions in narrative. Ask students to add transitions to the drafts they have read if these words will make the narrative more coherent and logical.

The following are answers to the exercises in Some Practice
with Transitions:

First paragraph:

Sentence 1:   plane (key word); and (conjunction of
               addition); first (conjunction of chronology);
               pilot (key word)
Sentence 2:   but (conjunction of contrast)
Sentence 3:   plane (key word); which (key word)
Sentence 4:   It (key word); about fifteen minutes
               (conjunction of chronology -key words); by
               which time (conjunction of chronology -key
               word); because (conjunction of cause)
Sentence 5:   But (conjunction of contrast); after
               (conjunction of chronology); a couple of
               minutes (key phrase); and (conjunction of
               addition)
Sentence 6:   pilot (key word)
Sentence 7:   and (conjunction of addition); pilot (key word)
Sentence 8:   and (conjunction of addition); followed by
               (conjunction of chronology)
Sentence 9:   them (key word); after (conjunction of
               chronology); a few seconds (key phrase); but
               (conjunction of contrast); plane (key word)

Second paragraph:

Sentence 1:   first (conjunction of chronology)
Sentence 2:   skiing (key word); right away (conjunction of
               chronology); but (conjunction of contrast);
               walk (key word); all over again (key phrase)
Sentence 3:   strapped (key word); boots (key word)
Sentence 4:   Because (conjunction of cause) boots (key
               word); straighten my legs (key phrase)
Sentence 5:   walking (key word); them (key word)
Sentence 6:   They (conjunction of chronology); skis (key
               word)
Sentence 7:   After (conjunction of chronology); them (key
               word); coordination (key word); legs and feet
               (key phrase)
Sentence 8:   At least (conjunction of emphasis);
               coordination (key word)
Sentence 10:   sneakers (key word)

The Halloween Party

Suggestions for adding transitions:

My friend decided to have a Halloween party on the Saturday

27

before Halloween. Because I was invited, I had to decide on what
costume I would wear, so I went to Rubie's Costume Rental and
picked out a Minnie Mouse costume.

I was especially excited about this party because everyone
would be wearing costumes. In fact, costume parties always seem
to be lively, for the disguises are usually amusing, funny, scary,
or creative, making the party interesting. And it can be fun to
be surrounded by imaginative figures. In addition, each person's
identity is disguised, and it's easy to play practical jokes on
each other. Because my costume disguised me from head to toe, no
one would know my real identity.

Finally Saturday night came, and I got dressed in my costume
and headed over to the party. The house was full of people in
their Halloween costumes, and my friends could not recognize me
under my mask. After awhile I had to identify myself to each one
of them.

Then I noticed someone wearing a Mickey Mouse costume who was
taking pictures of some of the people at the party. Soon he
noticed me in my Minnie Mouse costume and motioned me to come
over. He handed his camera to someone wearing a Peter Pan costume
so that Peter Pan could take a picture of Mickey and me together.
After all, Mickey and Minnie Mouse are a pair. After he thanked
me for being in the photograph with him, I left the picture-taking
scene to find my friends. But I wondered who it was wearing the
Mickey Mouse costume. Because he'd said only two words to me, I
hadn't recognized his voice.

Soon after, I saw an old friend of mine who happened to look
really cute in a Little Bo-Peep outfit, so I went over to talk to
her for a while. A short time after, we decided to look for more
of our friends. We found them on the dance floor and joined them.
When Mickey Mouse, who happened to be dancing away on the floor,
spotted me, he came over and we danced together. Although
everybody was working up a good sweat, I got tired after dancing
to a couple of songs, so I went to get something to drink.

The movie Halloween was being played on a VCR in the TV room,
and I decided to watch it. By the time the movie was over, it had
got rather late. As I started to clean up the house while my
friend broke up the party, I happened to turn around and catch
Mickey Mouse without his mask on, for he was saying goodnight to
some people. To my surprise, I found that the man under the
Mickey Mouse mask was my ex-boyfriend, the same ex-boyfriend that
I usually feel uncomfortable around and try to avoid.

Actually, our relationship had been a good one until he had
to move to Florida with his family. The day he left for Florida
was a sad one, and for awhile we wrote each other letters twice a
week. Also, we called each other on the phone at least once a
week. But after the first month, our communications grew less
frequent.

Although four months had passed, I had received only two
short letters from him. Then I got a call from him. He told me

28

that he would be moving back to New York within the next few months. I was _so_ extremely happy to think that I would be with him again _that_ I counted the days until he moved back to New York.

However, after he had moved back here, I realized that our relationship had changed. _Since_ he treated me as a friend instead of as a girlfriend, I realized that we no longer had a romantic relationship, _and_ I felt foolish; _therefore_, I decided to avoid him whenever possible.

But my experience with him at the Halloween party made me realize that there is no need for me to feel foolish or uncomfortable with him, _for_ the masks we wore helped me to relate to him as a person rather than as an ex-boyfriend. Feeling foolish was no longer an excuse for me to avoid him; it is okay to feel for him as a friend. _As a result_, I looked back at our relationship and was able to accept the change that had taken place.

Therefore, ending my relationship with him as a girlfriend did not end it as a friend. _In fact_, I had not been a friend to him because of fear that rejection of me as a girlfriend had affected his attitude toward me as a person. _Nor_ did it mean rejection of friendship, _for_ I now want a friendly relationship, like the one we had the night of the party.

Because images, impressions, fears, perceptions, and feelings toward others affect our relationships, we may see only one side of a situation or a person. _Yet_ the outside world can be very misleading about the real inside world that we live in and know. _For_ when we are disguised, our fears and anxieties, perceptions and worries are put aside. _Thus_ we can be ourselves and learn to see another side of the world we live in or of the people we know. If we look closely enough, _moreover_, we can see ourselves.

Rewriting

The Audience Response Guide is best used as part of peer group discussion. Students will usually share narratives quite enthusiastically and often have perceptive comment on the effectiveness of the essays they hear. They may be reluctant at first to make any specific changes in their peers' papers, but if you stress that their groups are for mutual encouragement and collaboration, they should shed their inhibitions quite soon.

The writer of "Approaching Life From a New Perspective" responded to the comments of his peers by adding details of his perceptions and reactions in paragraphs 4-6; along with a new introduction and conclusion, these help the writer "relive" the incident and help explain his point of view to the readers. He also adds information about his friend, to this effect. The addition of transitions such as _At that moment_ (conjunction of chronology) and _I realized_ (key phrase) in paragraph 6 improve the essay's coherence.

The primary element for establishing a grade for this task might be the effectiveness of the narrative--the authenticity of the voice, the use of concrete details, the establishment of some significance for the event written about. A secondary element might be the writer's skill in arranging narrative details, including the use of transitions.

Becoming Aware of Yourself as a Writer

Questions 1 - 3 ask students about their response to the journalist's questions and audience material. Questions 4 - 7 ask them to ponder the results of their writing on the task in light of the process that the chapter has asked them to follow.

CHAPTER FOUR: WRITING ABOUT A PLACE--EXPLORING YOUR POINT OF
                VIEW

     While we do not lose sight of the expressive element in all
the writing tasks in Ways to Writing, we emphasize the distinction
between expressive and expository writing in the Introduction to
"Part II: Exploration" so that students will understand the
different impulses behind them. Chapter 4 will retain many
expressive elements as will Chapter 5 and to varying extents
Chapters 6 to 11. But with our analogy of the baseball umpire and
his "limited" view of plays, we hope to dramatize for students the
difference between the single view and the multiple. Both
Chapters 4 and 5 expressly encourage students to seek this
multiple viewpoint, either through their seeking multiple
perspectives or through multiple observations. In this way, Part
II serves as a bridge between the largely expressive, subjective
aim of Part I: Self-Expression and the more traditional research
and expository qualities of Part III: Explanation (Chs. 6 and 7).

                         ******

     The task for this chapter is to acquire some first-hand
information about a place; students are thus introduced to methods
of primary research. While the task involves some of the
activities of the traditional descriptive essay, much more is
demanded of students. Not only must they visit and describe the
physical appearance of their chosen site, but they must also
observe any activity occurring and interview someone knowledgeable
about the place, using several questions of a heuristic (the
tagmemic) aimed at rooting out information about an unfamiliar
subject. While the student does not disappear from the written
results of this task--he or she will narrate his or her visit and
evaluate the place--the task requires the student to explore an
unfamiliar subject and present the results of his or her research
in an objective fashion.

Purpose

     We urge students in this chapter to shift their
responsibility from a concern to express themselves and their
experience, albeit with an ear to the ground for the reader's
response, to a concern to thoroughly explore their subject and to
present information about it in such a way that the reader will
understand it.

     The teacher might want to underline this transition by asking
the student to write briefly about a personal experience from his
or her point of view, and then to write about the experience as
other people might view it--those involved directly or

peripherally. A third paragraph combining all points of view--the writer's as well as others'--will approach the subject more thoroughly and more objectively. The third paragraph does not replace the first: they both are legitimate reactions to the experience, and one is preferable to the other only as the writer's aim changes.

This is a good time to emphasize the value of field research. The example of Honest Sam's Used Cars can lead to a fruitful discussion of objective exploration of multiple points of view.

Task: Exploring a Place

As we indicated in our introduction to the chapter above, the task for Chapter 4 has many components: the student is asked to visit a place, arrange for an interview, generate the answers to five questions, arrange the answers in three modes (narration, description, exposition) plus dialogue, write for an informed peer audience, and evaluate the place. While this may appear to be overly complex, in fact students tend to complete this task more successfully than some others, probably because of the concreteness and obvious practicality of the subject matter.

Their major hurdle is to decide on a place, arrange the visit, and find time to go. You will probably want to give students at least two, perhaps three weeks to complete this task. You will want to give them a chance to discuss possible places with their peer groups, and some students will want you to discuss other possibilities with them in conference. Occasionally, we have found ourselves involved in the process of arranging a visit, particularly to places on campus which may require faculty intervention, such as the data processing center. In addition to all its other good qualities, this task gives students practice in presenting themselves to others, usually professional people.

The idea for this task came originally from James Moffett (see Bibliography) who in turn borrowed it from The New Yorker's "Reporter at Large" column. We have found that many of the "Talk of the Town" columns in The New Yorker also illustrate the task very well. In fact, as Saul Bellow's essay on the kibbutz below demonstrates, the task suggests components, including the heuristic questions, found in much professional writing on a place or activity.

We have also used the film Before the First Word, distributed by Encyclopedia Britannica, in conjunction with this task as an introduction to the concept of student as reporter.

Writing Your Essay

Students find the "Explorer's Questions" very helpful in conducting their interviews. Not only can they not always locate the answers to Questions 2-5 through mere observation, but the questions also give them something intelligent to ask the interviewee. If sufficiently involved in the type of place they are visiting, students will also generate their own questions as well. If visiting a place related to their career choice, for example, they often question the people they meet there about their career choice.

Since students are again writing to their peers (see Chs. 2 and 3), you might want to encourage them to locate an actual group--a class or a group of aficionados for their hobby or interest--so that they will distinguish between writing for one group of peers and another. Ostensibly, they would shape a different essay for this more informed group than for their English class, the audience for Chapter 3. They might go into greater depth with less background, use a more technical vocabulary, and utilize the voice of one explorer writing to another. They should complete the Audience Analysis Guide so that their group can role-play this more expert audience as they critique their essays. While it is impossible through role-play to acquire information you do not possess, the peer group member can question the writer when necessary to determine level and clarity of information presented.

In arranging the narrative sections of the essay, students will be writing a narrative of what always happens (process analysis in response to explorer's question 5) inside a narrative of what happened once (their visit to the place). A lesson on verb tenses can be inserted here as the simple past can be used to narrate the visit, and the present tense to narrate the process.

The responses to the explorer's questions 2-4 clearly call for exposition and give students further experience in distinguishing it from narration. As in Ch. 3, the student is asked to explain the subject and also to step back further and evaluate the subject for an overriding impression.

Generating Ideas: The Explorer's Questions. In attempting to utilize Young, Becker, and Pike's tagmemic heuristic devised from their study of linguistics (in Rhetoric: Discovery and Change--see Bibliography below), we discovered that Ross Winterowd had presented a very effective approach in his The Contemporary Writer (see Bibliography). From the original nine-cell matrix, Winterowd has culled the five questions that we present in this chapter.

This question set is essentially new and, we have found, very useful for inquiry into the unfamiliar and unknown, as opposed to the classical questions (Chs. 5-7), which speculate about the known. We compare and contrast the purposes of these two sets of questions in Chapter 5.

Exercise 1 under Some Practice with the Explorer's Questions encourages students to try the question set in their journal.

Exercises 2 and 3 are fun but at the same time call for a bit of ingenuity and creativity in completing them. Furthermore, Exercise 3 again demonstrates, as should Exercise 2, how thoroughly these questions explore a subject. Exercise 2 also reveals the common sense quality of the inquiry as the dialogue is not so far removed from that which takes place in such situations.

Exercise 4 starts the student seriously on the explorer's path by asking her or him to adopt first the role of market researcher and then the role of academic investigator, as does Exercise 2 under Some Practice with Using the Explorer's Questions to Generate Ideas About a Place.

Exercise 1 under Some Practice with Using the Explorer's Questions to Generate Ideas About a Place invites students to try out the question set on a place that they have visited in the past. Students may not, of course have explored the place sufficiently to answer all five questions about it, but their very lack of information should indicate to them how inadequate mere observation usually is and how useful the question set will prove to be. This realization will prepare them to explore the place for the chapter task more thoroughly.

The journal works nicely as a double-entry notebook while students explore a place. They take notes on the left-hand side as they conduct their field research, then on the right-hand side react to, analyze and assess the answers to the explorer's questions that they have collected.

Addressing Your Audience: Depth of Information. Since students will be writing their various expository tasks for audiences of differing educational levels, analyzing the qualities--the facts presented, the details, the vocabulary, the allusions, the definitions and explanation--of passages written by professional writers for audiences of various backgrounds will aid students in determining how to tailor their own writing for different readers.

You may wish to add to or substitute for the passages on preparation other passages geared to audiences with different backgrounds on a subject. Another good source would be medical books--those for lay people and those for doctors or researchers. Or students might be interested in how far they have progressed in their education by comparing one of their current textbooks with a high school text on the same subject.

The exercises at the end of this section are fairly straightforward; you may want to ask students to outline the article for each audience for Exercise 3 (or the two letters for Exercise 1). Exercise 2 asks the student to actually write two letters for different audiences.

Peer group discussion of the exercises under Some Practice in Determining Your Audience's Depth of Information for Your Essay on a Place should help students move into the rough draft stage of writing their essay on a place.

<u>Arranging</u> <u>Your</u> <u>Essay.</u> Saul Bellow's essay "On a Kibbutz" illustrates how this task, with all its apparent complexities, might be approached. Students can see that the various features of the kibbutz are mentioned and/or described throughout the essay as Bellow makes his morning tour: the children's dormitory, the rows of small kibbutz dwellings, the sea, the citrus and banana groves, the Roman ruins including the Herodian Hippodrome, the tile factory, the barn, the dining hall, a basketball court, the separate quarters for young women of eighteen, and a museum of antiquities. His description of his walk among the fruit groves and Roman ruins evokes many of the senses.

The Kibbutz appears to operate as a self-supporting community with parents freed from child care to work at the various occupations. Since he provides little background, he evidently is writing for a reader familiar with the kibbutz.

While Bellow does not compare the kibbutz to other kibbutzim, he does refer to other orange-exporting countries and to the competition among them, thus placing the Israeli kibbutz into one of its several classes.

The kibbutzniks have endured war--the son of his friend, John, was killed in the Golan; terrorists and Turks have attacked on the sea and even the beaches so that they are all armed--and Lebanon is being destroyed to the north by Arab militants, particularly Syrians who also threaten Israel. The threat of war and death permeates their lives and reminds the author that paradise can be quickly lost.

John's life as a German Jew during World War II is alluded to: the prologue to his hopes for Israel and the kibbutz life. However, the wars with the Arabs have tempered those hopes, as on John's desk stands a framed photograph of his dead son. There is no more fishing on the kibbutz, and on the beaches there are now armed patrols. Despite the daily fear, John and his wife maintain a cheerful front.

Bellow has obviously found the kibbutz to be an exquisite place in terms of its geography and the emotional lives of its inhabitants. His overriding impression, found in the last line of the essay: "What is there to keep them from blowing away?", underscores the lovely but precarious kibbutz existence.

Paul Engle's descriptive essay on the Iowa State Fair offers another approach to writing on a place, emphasizing the process of the Fair. Students can determine whether or not the Fair seems "corny" through Engle's energetic approach.

The student essay "Paying for a Higher Education" shows students that it is possible for them to approximate Bellow's approach to the task. In his first 2 paragraphs, the student combines narration and description in his introduction to his visit to NYU. His 3rd paragraph, in answer to explorer's question 5 about the parts of the place (its crowds of people), fits exposition smoothly into his narrative. Paragraphs 1-4 also respond to the explorer's question 3 by detailing how NYU fits into its Greenwich Village neighborhood. The next five paragraphs (5-9) interweave the narrative of his visit with the process that a student must go through and with a descriptive analysis of different parts of NYU (question 5). In paragraph 8, the student answers question 2 by implicitly comparing NYU to other schools. He concludes the essay with a statement of his overriding impression.

You might want your students to evaluate the essay at this point using the "Audience Response Guide."

Focus on Form: Paragraph Development/Writing a Conclusion

Paragraph Development. This section, based on Francis Christensen's "A Generative Rhetoric of the Paragraph" (see Bibliography below), illustrates how structure can induce thought. By consciously adopting one of Christensen's strategies for structuring a paragraph, students learn to distinguish among levels of abstraction. This approach to paragraph structure reinforces the student's sense, developed in various ways throughout the book, of the difference between the general and the specific, and how to move from one to the other with some ease.

Outlining paragraphs to discover their structure, whether it be coordinate, subordinate, or some combination of the two, also provides students with a simplified approach to learning to see the framework of a larger piece of writing and of learning to

frame their own work, whether done as a prewriting step or after
the rough draft has been written.

The structure of Marya Mannes's paragraph is coordinate; she
lists reasons why commercials are supposedly in the public
interest. By paraphrasing her sentences, students should be able
to see easily the parallel generalizations. Petrunkevitch's
paragraph, on the other hand, proceeds by subordinating nearly
every successive sentence to the one preceding it. Chief Joseph
presents a mixed structure that might be outlined thus:

1. Tell General Howard I know his heart.
2. What he told me before I have in my heart.
3. I am tired of fighting.
   4. Our Chiefs are killed.
      5. Looking Glass is dead.
      6. Toohoolhoolzote is dead.
      7. The old men are all dead.
         8. It is the young men who say yes or no.
      9. He who led on the young men (Ollokot) is dead.
10. My people, some of them, have run away to the hills, and
have no blankets, no food; no one knows where they are--perhaps
freezing to death.
11. I want to have time to look for my children and see how many
of them I can find.
   12. Maybe I shall find them among the dead.
13. Hear me, my chiefs! I am tired; my heart is sick and sad.
14. From where the sun now stands I will fight no more forever.

Trippet's paragraph is also mixed, following this structure:

1.   It is thus no exaggeration to say that Americans have taken
to mechanical cooling avidly and greedily.
      2. Many have become all but addicted, refusing to go places
that are not air-conditioned.
         3. In Atlanta, shoppers in Lenox Square so resented having
         to endure natural heat while walking outdoors from chilled
         store to chilled store that the mall management enclosed
         and air-conditioned the whole sprawling shebang.
         4. The widespread whining about Washington's raising of
         thermostats to a mandatory 78 degrees F suggests that
         people no longer think of interior coolness as an amenity
         but consider it a necessity, almost a birthright, like
         suffrage.
         5. The existence of such a view was proved last month when
         a number of federal judges sitting too high and mighty to
         suffer 78 degrees F, defied and denounced the Government's
         energy-saving order to cut back on cooling.
            6. Significantly, there was no popular outrage at this
            judicial insolence; many citizens probably wished that

37

they could be so highhanded.

As their methods of exposition, Mannes used "reasons why," Petrunkevitch used process analysis, Chief Joseph also listed reasons why, and Trippet cited examples.

Writing a Conclusion. You might choose to introduce the material on writing a conclusion in Chapter 2, particularly if you want to compare introductory and concluding strategies. We have included this section here, because the task for Chapter 3 requires a strong conclusion that sums up or explains the overriding impression that the process of exploring a place has made on the writer.

Rewriting

In utilizing the "Audience Response Guide" for this task, students will want to look for the writer's statement of his or her overriding impression in answering question 1, for an adequate depth of information for the intended audience for question 2, and for a successful integration to the modes and answers to the explorer's questions in question 3. The answer to question 4 will steer the writer to adding any missing information, rearranging the answers to the questions for smoother flow, or substituting the appropriate depth of information or method of development for that used when necessary.

In revising his essay, the writer of "Paying for a Higher Education" adds some descriptive details of the NYU campus, such as its "stately brick and stone buildings" in paragraph 4. He also adds to the dialogue in paragraph 4, perhaps to convey a more complex sense of his impression of the school.

In paragraph 7, he elaborates on the film school's reputation as well as its cost, thus developing his response to explorer's question 2; and he adds the sentence that begins "The seeds of doubt," clarifying his initial expectations and so his final impression--which he explains in more detail in his last paragraph.

Perhaps he substitutes "So it's better not to be caught staring" for "It happens more often than you think" in response to his peers' suggestion that he keep in mind those readers who may be unfamiliar with New York; perhaps he makes this substitution simply to keep the focus more firmly on himself and his impressions.

Students can compare this revision with their own.

<u>Becoming</u> <u>Aware</u> <u>of</u> <u>Yourself</u> <u>as</u> <u>a</u> <u>Writer</u>

These questions ask the student to consider various aspects of the writing process just completed as well as how to utilize what they have learned in future writing situations.

CHAPTER FIVE: WRITING ABOUT A PREJUDGMENT--EXPLORING OTHER POINTS
               OF VIEW

From our experience in assigning students the tasks presented
in Ways to Writing, the task in this chapter is in several ways
the most difficult, perhaps because it requires the most
introspective and self-analytic thinking at the same time that it
demands careful observation and awareness of change over a period
of time.   Students are asked to write a case--to examine a
situation about which they have formed a prejudgment--and to test
that opinion through the acquisition of evidence.   They must
collect this evidence during the course of a number of visits to a
place, or through several observations of events or persons.

Students take on the role of investigator, moving beyond
their own experience into the community to subject their knowledge
to evidence that they themselves have gathered.   We don't suggest
that students change their original view of a subject, only that
they submit it to disinterested, objective observation.   Once they
realize that a prejudice is a state of mind or attitude from which
learning can take place, they respond quite enthusiastically.   It
is important, of course, to clarify that we have prejudices about
many things, and therefore that students do not have to feel
threatened that they may have to examine, for example, their
feelings about other people.

One advantage of the case approach is that it draws on the
students' problem-solving abilities, asking them to create a kind
of dialectic between what they already assume to be true and what
the evidence they collect may indicate is more likely the truth.
The result can be a new synthesis of reasoned judgment and
detached observation.   In the process of pursuing the task,
students may have to reject a hypothesis and create a new one.   We
make the analogy of a scientist investigating a subject, and this
points ahead to Chapter 10, where students will write an
investigative paper on a topic drawn from the sciences or social
sciences.   As they write this task, they can learn that writing is
not merely the recording of facts already arrived at, but an
active form of learning in itself.

Realizing that this task would require a heuristic of
substance and flexibility, we found in the Aristotelian topics a
method students can easily adapt to their investigations.   By
using what we call the classical questions, students learn about
cause and effect, analogy, comparison and contrast, and process
analysis through the pursuit of their case study.

Because this task requires students to explore other possible
points of view, we have also asked them to identify a broad public

audience that would be interested in reading about their case. And as a source for actual publication, we pose the possibility of preparing an essay for a more local outlet such as a newsletter.

Purpose

This task challenges students' fundamental psychic conditioning. Like all of us, they make snap judgments, hold past patterns of behavior to be etched permanently in stone, and generalize without much supporting evidence. What a surprise then that we ask them to submit their own mental process to investigation along with the topic they choose. We find that this task arouses some of the most energetic and purposeful group work. You might divide them into groups just after you explain the purpose of this chapter, asking them to consider some of those prejudices that even the most educated among us fall easy prey to; for example, popular movies are fated to find even less demanding audiences, the beloved National Parks are destined to be engulfed by discarded beer cans and junked recreation vehicles, and city people are less friendly than people in suburban or rural areas.

Students will enjoy sharing your own personal list of ironclad prejudgments and will most assuredly make recommendations as to how best to submit them to examination. You might want to share as well your methods for overcoming the tendency to make prejudgments: i.e., how does an educated person face the inadequacy of his or her own mental patterns? One way is through the case method, for it allows us to gather evidence upon which we can either confirm or reject our original point of view.

Task: Writing About a Prejudgment

Students first must clearly understand what a prejudgment is--that it is coming to a conclusion with precious little, if any, factual support. Any topic they may suggest must be one that they have not yet gathered facts about or that they have no substantial reason for inferring the outcome of. The situation must be one that they can observe frequently, or, if they wish to prejudge the outcome--the performance of a team or a theatrical group, for example--the outcome must occur within the time in which they are doing the observing.

The key to eliciting some effective papers for this task is in showing students the dynamic nature of the case as it develops over a period of several visits. It isn't easy for them to envisage a gradual change or development in a subject. Several class or group discussions may be necessary before students feel confident enough to forge ahead.

Another purpose of this task is to draw students further away from writing narratives and give them more guidance in the essential methods of exposition: analysis, causation, comparison and contrast, and process. We find it a good idea to show students how narrative has its limits and that it must serve in this task, as in Chapter 4, merely as a chronological framework for the interpretive elements they wish to emphasize.

We encourage students to pursue relatively offbeat subjects for this task. Because they tend to hold rather grim attitudes toward the notion of prejudice or prejudgment, we have found that asking them to behold such mental tendencies in commonplace acts or everyday situations is a good way to allay their fears about revealing themselves as raging bigots or provincials. If a student questions whether examining a prejudice about the flimsiness of American cars is a substantial topic, we emphasize that there is much to learn in writing on this subject. In effect, he is about to pursue research through interviewing some new car owners and making several visits to car dealerships in his neighborhood. By the time he completes the task, he will have accomplished several complex writing and thinking activities.

Writing the Essay

Generating Ideas: The Classical Questions. The great advantage of the Aristotelian topics for the writer--underlined by their being used for over two thousand years--is that they actually work. Students often have difficulty getting started on expository essays, and the classical questions give them a beginning for virtually any subject (although, as we have noted in Chapter 4, the explorer's questions work well with open-ended inquiry, and they may be utilized here in combination with the classical questions). We have combined the task--an active, dynamic form of arriving at a conclusion--with the strategies of classical rhetoric--generally a static mode of investigation--to form a writing process that can give students confidence in approaching a subject that at the outset appears quite problematic.

We often ask students to name a subject they have considered but aren't sure about. We then put it on the blackboard and try to work out an approach to it through the classical questions. This is quite effective in getting them over their initial reservations about the task.

The exercises in Some Practice with the Classical Questions point out some of the absurd possibilities in our tendency to ascribe causes to certain effects. It will be clear that they pose serious errors in commonplace logic; some of them we've heard or seen elsewhere in more important contexts. For Exercise 3, you may wish to substitute more timely comparisons or contrasts of your own.

Addressing Your Audience: Writing for Publication. You may want to bring to class some examples of the publications mentioned in this section. You might ask those students with specialized interests to provide copies of their favorite magazine and explain the nature of its audience. This might also be a profitable short exercise for group discussion.

Local and student newspapers and specialized magazines can indeed be a possible source for publication although, realistically, publication cannot be the primary purpose of the task for this chapter. We find that students are well aware of the different audiences for various publications but are not very conscious of the rhetorical effects and subtle appeals that magazines, in particular, make to their readers.

Arranging the Essay. You might ask some students to duplicate for the whole class their answers to four classical questions that they have asked about the prejudgment that they are testing. We remind students at this point that they are actually preparing to organize their essay and that they should try to determine what arrangement pattern is best for the material they have generated.

We ask students to bring to class a copy of the publication they have in mind as the outlet for their essay. For the student writing on the flimsiness of American cars, we suggested a local newspaper or consumer newsletter. We then ask students to write a brief response to the Audience Analysis Guide with the model publication at hand. For group discussion, we pass the response and the publication around in order to familiarize the rest of the group with the publication. Then, we ask them to role-play the audience for this publication and to comment on the appropriateness of the intended article.

You may have to offer specific suggestions to students as to how patterns of cause and effect, comparison and contrast, and process analysis can be developed from the material they have generated. For comparison and contrast, for example, you might illustrate on the blackboard a topic developed by both whole-by-whole and part-by-part methods and ask students to choose the more effective example.

Richard Rodriguez's autobiographical essay highlights many of the benefits to be gained from the writing of a case. Although the essay is cast in narrative form, the author analyzes his relationship to the other workers and eventually to los pobres during his summer spent in strenuous physical labor, observes both groups keenly, and derives a deepened understanding of his fellow workers and the Mexican laborers that would permanently alter his social consciousness. By tracing his changing views over the course of a summer, Rodriguez also compares his status as a worker to that of the Mexicans. By doing this, he begins to see their individuality, but even more so, he sees his distance from the anonymity of the aliens whose poverty and hopelessness he could never come to understand.

In his essay on Allen Ginsberg, Patrick Fenton moved through several stages in his prejudgment of the poet. From an adolescent worship of Ginsberg, he moved to a middle-aged suspicion of him. Not until he actually had the opportunity to conduct several interviews of the man was he able to arrive at a reasoned judgment, one unlike either of his prejudgments.

Fenton, like Rodriguez, uses a narrative framework on which he builds other arrangement patterns such as explanation and description.

Writing Your Rough Draft. The student writer of the rough draft in this section, like Rodriguez and Fenton, inserts description, explanation, and contrast into her narrative of her case of the values of listening to classical music.

Focus: Sentence Combining

Sentence combining has emerged in recent years as one of the most useful ways to build more expressive sentences and solve problems of punctuation and sentence rhythm and variety as well. We have compressed a good deal of information in this chapter section from Glenn J. Broadhead and James A. Berlin's "Twelve Steps to Using Generative Sentences and Sentence Combining in the Composition Classroom" (see Bibliography below). You may want to consider all or part of this section here or refer to it in later chapters. You might also find it helpful to refer to the Focus section of Chapter 3 on transitions.

The Summary Exercise can be answered in many ways. You may want to have your students work on it in groups and then compare results. Here is one possible combination although you may suggest that students alter the wording of the original sentences more than has been done here.

IMAGINARY JANE

When I moved into the house we bought from my grandfather, and which we are still living in now, I was only three years old. Because other families living on my block were mostly old people and their children were grown up, there were no other children to

44

play with, which left me no choice but to play by myself.

Finding many things to do on my own, I would play house and dolls alone. I played with my parents but they were often too busy; therefore, the day was really long and boring. This went on for a couple of years until kindergarten started. Because I made new friends and had a lot of classmates, school was a relief.

This did not, of course, help me with my problem of staying alone, for I continued to stay by myself at home. When I became six, a little girl named Diane moved next door, but being so used to staying alone, I did not like to play with her. Because I was afraid she was going to take my toys away from me, I did not want her to touch any of my things.

But staying alone was not such a good idea. I started to make things up, pretending I had an imaginary friend named Jane. Not knowing anyone with that name, I have no idea where it came from. However, Jane lived in the bathroom and in many of the closets around the house, and I talked to her, pretending that she answered me.

When we would play house together, my mother would give me cookies and milk. I, of course, ate my cookies, but so did Jane. This playing with Jane until I went to bed in the evening went on for about a whole year.

Finally, my parents began to get worried and asked my doctor about Jane, this imaginary friend. The doctor said it was normal for a lonely child to create an imaginary friend but made a recommendation that I should play with a real friend, Diane.

Because my mother made me play with Diane, I would call for her and we would play together for a little while. Playing with Diane all the time, little by little I forgot about Jane. I have rarely thought about Jane again until now, for this essay. Although this went on for a whole year, it was not an unusual phase to go through.

Rewriting

You might have students analyze each of the questions in the Audience Response Guide, perhaps adding specifics as they do so. Comparing their responses to "A Classical Question" with those of our students will reinforce the variety of reader perceptions. You may want your students to evaluate the final draft of the student essay as well, using either the Audience Response Guide or the Checklist of Questions to Consider. Students might examine the final draft of the student essay for additional possibilities for distributing, for example: Would distributing additional contrasts between classical and rock music have been useful?

You might also want students to review the other revision strategies presented in earlier chapters: cutting, adding, rearranging, substituting. They might phrase additional questions about these strategies to add to the Checklist before revising

their own essays. Examining the student's revision of "A
Classical Question" for each of these strategies should reinforce
the revision process for students.

Becoming Aware of Yourself as a Writer

        The questions direct students to think about the case
approach and other aspects of the task they have completed.
Question 5 asks them to consider the classical and explorer's
questions as heuristics for future thinking and writing.
Questions 1 and 4 may be enriched by group discussion.

CHAPTER SIX: WRITING ABOUT A TRADITION--EXPLAINING WHAT YOU KNOW

The distinction made in the Introduction to Part III between the aims of exploration and explanation prepares the student for the tasks in Chapters 6 and 7. Discussing the Introduction is worth a few moments of class time.

In Chapters 6 and 7, we ask students to move beyond the acts of exploring the world outside themselves that they engaged in while completing the tasks for Chapters 4 and 5. Now, their tasks are to explain subjects with which they are already familiar and to more generalized audiences: the uninformed reader in Chapter 6 and a more or less defined segment of the larger society in Chapter 7. These tasks require a broader perspective, a greater consciousness of the need to generalize about values and ideas that are inherent in their subject and to be able to convey them to readers in an appropriate public voice. As a result of completing these tasks, students' writing should become more informative in content and more authoritative in voice.

Chapters 6 and 7 continue, of course, many of the aspects of writing introduced earlier. The use of the classical questions to generate ideas is developed further as new questions appropriate to the chapter tasks are presented. The use of generalization, introduced in earlier chapters through the development of a shaping idea, is amplified here as students seek to convey the sense of their information to their intended readers.

The task for this chapter provides students with a subject that they can explain to the reader without considerable research. In writing about a family or cultural tradition, they may solicit information from family documents or other family members, but they also may write solely from memory.

We think the relatively research-free tasks in this and the following chapter are important at this juncture in the text and in students' development as writers and thinkers for several reasons. One is that students need to realize that they are storehouses not only of personal experiences but also of objective information that they can draw on for a piece of writing. In explaining this information to a reader, they gain authority.

Chapters 6 and 7 thus correspond to the first three chapters in drawing upon students' own experience and knowledge, while the succeeding chapters parallel Chapters 4 and 5 in drawing upon field and/or library research.

Also, because we ask students to move from the narrative mode into the expository, a difficult transition for many students, a fairly uncomplicated task allows them to concentrate on developing the interplay between abstraction and concrete example that successful exposition requires.

Finally, students need to appreciate the cultural diversity of contemporary America both for their own self-development and esteem and for that of the culture. In introducing the task, you might ask students to discuss the following quotes:

"To be an American is forthrightly to acknowledge a collective identity that simultaneously transcends and encompasses our disparate identities and communities. Unless we acknowledge our diversity, we allow the silence of received tradition (about difference and inequality) to become our own." Elizabeth Fox-Genovese. Feminism Without Illusions. U. of N. Carolina Press, 1991.

"For all of our national faults and shortcomings, the United States is the most successful multi-ethnic and multiracial society of our time. If, as a nation, we are to continue to develop this great strength of ours, we must work toward an appreciation of differences within a common frame of shared values that transcends and harmonizes those differences." Raymond F. Bacchetti and Steven S. Weiner, chair and executive director of the Accrediting Commission for the Western Association of Schools and Colleges. "Diversity is a Key Factor in Educational Quality and Hence in Accreditation," Chronicle of Higher Education (1991).

Purpose

The aim of writing in this and the following chapter is to explain. Students are to explain a subject to an audience that is unfamiliar with it. This task turns the aim of most writing that students have done in their lives on its head. Rather than writing for someone (the teacher) who knows more than they do, students have an opportunity to become the teacher. Many types of writing students will encounter after completing their education will again provide them the opportunity to write as experts: technical manuals, reports, letters to their children, etc.

Students are also being asked to explain a cultural or family tradition to someone from a different tradition. This particular explanatory task, as we remind students in the purpose section, occurs often in our culture whenever the natural curiosity of a member of a different group prompts an explanation or in more formal situations when, for example, one group seeks permission of a school or public official for a celebration or demonstration of that tradition, in gathering, ceremony, or parade.

Still another aim of this task is to encourage students to learn about the traditions of others as we have indicated in the introduction above. As students share their family and cultural traditions in their groups and with the class in the process of writing the essay, they will learn about and hopefully appreciate the cultural diversity of the United States.

Task

The aspects of culture around which traditions have accumulated are numerous: family, race, religion, ethnicity, gender, class. An initial discussion of all of these areas is key if students are to understand their range of choices.

As we have indicated to students in the text, thoroughly assimilated Americans find it difficult to stand back from the flow of their lives and recognize distinct family or cultural patterns. These students tend to think that they are, well, just living life as it is supposed to be and that those from other cultures, religions, or races are somehow deviant. In the current jargon, the hegemony of the until recently majority culture has blinded its members to their own peculiarities.

Having students read Shelby Steele's description of the features of the American middle class in "On Being Black and Middle Class," one of the professional models in this chapter, and compare it with the comment of Henry Louis Gates below should help to carve the majority culture in bas-relief if not in sharp contrast. To Shelby Steele's perception that the American middle class is monolithic--"values and patterns of responsibility that are common to the middle class everywhere"--and his assertion that middle class blacks have more in common with middle class whites than with lower class blacks, Gates's belief in a "hyphenated culture" that would transcend class offers a counterpoint:

"To demand that Americans shuck their cultural heritage and homogenize themselves into an "universal" WASP culture is to dream of an America in cultural white face, and that just won't do.

"So it's only when we're free to explore the complexities of our hyphenated culture that we can discover what a genuinely common American culture might actually look like."

--Henry Louis Gates Jr. "Whose Culture Is It, Anyway?" the New York Times (1991).

Or, having Protestant students read Anna Quindlen's essay included here "I Am a Catholic" and list the differing characteristics of their religion that have framed their lives and traditions may assist them in seeing themselves as "Anglo-Americans."

For students with strong memories of other cultures, this task may elicit the profound insight and poetic imagery often the metier of the culturally divergent.

For all students, this exercise in comparative cultures is an educational one. "Culture is always a conversation among different voices." Henry Louis Gates Jr. (Times 1991)

Generating Ideas: At this point in the process for writing this essay, students should feel confident: they are the teacher in this task. Classroom atmosphere is important for the next step, which is brainstorming. If students are to take their own thoughts and those of others seriously, they must feel empowered. It is vital for you to be the facilitator of their brainstorming processes, whether listing or clustering.

The peer group also plays a role in generating ideas for this task. The respect of students for each other's traditions will encourage ideas; any lack of respect may stultify the generation process or at the least make explanation more difficult. What students learn from their group about what their potential readers know about the subject will also influence their depth of information choices.

Both brainstorming strategies should be used initially spontaneously to generate ideas. Because both are also effective in generating levels of abstraction--in organizing the essay--a second and third round of brainstorming can be conducted. While listing lends itself more readily to the linear outline, many students may be more sympathetic to the multi-directional visual opportunities provided by clustering. Clustering provides a freedom that listing does not.

Clustering (or its siblings, branching and constructing trees) also reinforces the distinctions between the concrete and the abstract, between idea and story, that successful explanation requires. To enhance the distinctions between levels of abstraction, different shapes may be given to each level: circle for main idea, rectangle for each supporting generalization, triangle for each story. Students may create their own clusters or you may even give them a cluster form to fill in. Clusters can be messy and at this organizing stage, the clarity of the visual construct is important.

50

Freewriting in their journal about past reenactments of the tradition may foster memory.

Many of the exercises in this section call for research such as consulting family documents and albums and interviewing or writing to family members. Another uses students' knowledge of family shows on television and still another, the students' knowledge of American history and related stories.

Audience. If your class is culturally diverse, then students will easily play the role of uninformed reader for each other. If your class is culturally homogenous in terms of class, race, ethnicity, and religion, students will still be uninformed about family or possibly even gender traditions. Students, of course, may choose other readers outside the class, in which case peers can role play the uninformed reader.

The exercises provide opportunities for students to practice explaining to an uninformed reader as well as adopting an appropriate tone. The assumption here is that students will not be writing a procedural manual to an objective audience, but because Americans are tentative about their cultural differences, an effort must be made to draw the reader into the subject by referring to her values and using a reassuring tone.

Arranging the Essay. Students are asked to form a shaping idea that indicates the aspects of the subject the essay will cover and their attitude toward it. Both student and professional shaping ideas are included for analysis.

Students are urged to maintain an objective distance from the tradition they are explaining; any personal reactions are to be representative of the family or cultural group. Two additional patterns of arrangement, definition and classification, are discussed with examples. Both patterns are particularly useful in fulfilling this task, which may in fact be an extended definition.

Storytelling fulfills the rhetorical need for concrete examples and is well-suited to this task. Stories of what happened once or of what always happens are both appropriate here. Because students often cannot move easily between stories and their significance, you may want to have students write the stories separately--before or after--explaining the significance of the tradition.

The model essays weave storytelling with explanation. Anna Quindlen's essay "I Am a Catholic" and "On Being Black and Middle Class" by Shelby Steele both contain stories, both of the "what happened once" and "what always happened" kind. Because Quindlen uses more stories than Steele with less exposition, you might seek students' responses to the value of more or fewer stories. The rough draft of the student essay "House of Delight" is largely narrative, telling the story of what always happened but including several one-time stories. Students might look at her revised version to see how she added some explanation.

Focus on Form and Style

Both explanatory and narrative writing lend themselves to wordiness, as we explain in the text, and students are urged to eliminate unnecessary words from their writing in drafting the essay for this task.

Another useful exercise for eliminating deadwood in addition to those we have included here is to ask students to cut any essay they have previously written in half. While this is an arbitrary amount to delete and may have to be modified, most students will find that their writing suffers little from omitting wasteful words.

Rewriting

In evaluating the task for this chapter, the primary traits to look for can be found in the first four questions of a "Checklist of Questions to Consider in Revising an Essay About a Tradition." Secondary traits may include question 5 on arrangement and the elimination of deadwood.

Becoming Aware of Yourself As a Writer

Students may want to share their answers to questions 1 and 2 in groups.

CHAPTER SEVEN: WRITING ABOUT THE MEDIA--EXPLAINING WHAT YOU THINK

In Chapter 7, as in Chapter 6, we ask students to explain a subject from a broad perspective, to generalize about values and ideas that are inherent in their subject. In this chapter, generalization is raised to the level of a heuristic: the student is asked to answer the classical question "What general ideas and values does the subject exemplify?" In Chapter 7 the student is, in effect, asked to perform a task in which rhetorical skills developed through all the previous tasks are specifically applied to writing the sort of literate, informed analysis associated with those essayists most often anthologized in rhetoric readers.

The Audience section features another important characteristic of the literate essay by asking students to write in a "public voice." Here, we seek to encourage students to become more conscious of the conventions of public discourse, to the attention they must pay to argument, decorum, and reasoned objectivity. Although Edwin Newman's views on language run counter to those of many writers, he writes without hectoring his audience or badgering them into accepting his position on the effects of television on language. The student can recognize that the author's audience is in large part responsible for this reasoned approach and the generalizations and examples that result.

Purpose

Perhaps a sense of purpose for this chapter can evolve from a discussion of the relationship between the consumer of media (reader, viewer) and the media themselves. What is the function of the media in a democratic society? What interpretive and evaluative stance should we expect from the consumer? What can be gained for ourselves and for the media by subjecting them to the examination we give them in this chapter? What kinds of information are most beneficial for the writer to convey? Students often have strong views about the manipulative intentions of the media and lump under "brainwashing" most of the persuasive machinery characteristic of print and visual media. Getting them to understand through class discussion how their knowledge of the media can contribute to the real, interpretive process necessary in a democratic society can itself be a valuable function of this chapter's task.

Task: Writing About the Media

In introducing the task for Chapter 7, you may need to elicit from students some evidence that they know more than they may think they do about the media. Some discussion of their viewing and reading habits and the range and extent of their media experiences should reassure them that they possess an ample fund of materials to draw from. This task requires them to become aware of themselves as media consumers, to note their own responses to the media's special forms of allure.

From some initial discussion, you might then move to the crucial role of interpretation in evaluating these experiences. Some students are not quite prepared at this stage to take the necessary inductive leap to make some generalization about, say, the trivialized lives of teenagers as they are represented in some sitcoms. You might ask them to describe brief vignettes from some of these shows and then to sum up the purpose or effect of these scenes in characterizing adolescent Americans.

To what degree a student's evaluating of the media takes on an argumentative tone is an issue here. We feel there is an argumentative component to any explanation. You may prefer to deemphasize this component, or you may encourage students to be argumentative to some degree and perhaps even have them look at the Focus section in Chapter 8, which deals with persuasive language.

In introducing the audience for the task, you might discuss the different kinds of television audiences, perhaps taking an informal poll of your students. We try not to be judgmental--at least not excessively--about some of their viewing habits that run counter to our own, but giving students a chance to express some of their preferences and aversions prepares them to address an audience of their own selection in a manner appropriate for what they expect this audience to share with them in knowledge and point of view.

Writing the Essay

Generating Ideas Through Generalization. In this section, students are encouraged to build on what they have already seen or heard through their experience with the media and to give substance and credibility to their experiences by formulating generalizations that would inform an audience familiar with these media. The relationship between supporting example and general statement is crucial to all thinking, as well as any academic writing, that students might encounter. By grounding the generalization in experiences that come easily to mind, we hope that students will achieve fluency in explaining what they know to others.

We begin with narrative examples because they are so pervasive in the world of the media where everything is seen as a "story." You might want to offer examples of your own--current "stories" in the news that can be shaped into a significant generalization, or trends in the media that need to be interpreted. From our experience, students often display a broad, far-ranging interest in nearly all aspects of the media; this can easily be brought to bear in a discussion of how crucial the act of generalizing is to the acquisition of knowledge and interpretive skills.

The exercises in this section are intended to help students tap their knowledge of the media and the opinions of others and to formulate a generalization about which they might write. Exercise 3 on p. 274 asks students to consider a generalization about John Wayne that needs to be interpreted and supported with specific examples. You might substitute other film starts and discuss what kind of generalization might be created from the values they exemplify.

Addressing Your Audience: Adopting a Public Voice. This section seeks to create in students a sensitivity to different forms of public expression. Students rarely focus their attention on the subtle interplay of writer and audience, but particularly when the media are discussed, the writer's public voice will be partly shaped and formulated by the education, values, and sophistication of the audience. You might want to compare Edwin Newman's voice with Alice McDermott's or Lewis Grossberger's, or perhaps with a media critic from your local newspaper. The range of public voices is, of course, remarkably extensive, and you might want to collect some notable ones that offer revealing and even entertaining contrasts.

By stressing that a public voice differs from a private voice mainly in degree, we try not to create a false sense of rift in the two voices, but mainly to emphasize how audience and subject impose structural and stylistic considerations on all writers.

The exercises in this section encourage students to become more aware of the nature and appropriateness of the public voices they are most likely to encounter. Exercise 1 on p. 282 asks them to recast a personal narrative and then to generalize about it. Exercise 2 focuses on the editorial articles of writers with strongly held beliefs that must still, however, be adapted to a more catholic audience. How the writer takes into account this distance between his or her own views and those of the audience is the subject of this exercise.

Exercise 3 considers the spoken public voice and can be expanded to include the public styles of a variety of well-known public figures. Exercise 4 is directed toward the peculiar phenomenon of TV anchor reporters. You might want to elicit from students some description of different anchor styles, ranging from the bland to the blatant, or whatever applies in your particular viewing community. Exercise 5 asks students to analyze the audiences of <u>New</u> <u>York</u> <u>Magazine</u> and <u>The</u> <u>Progressive</u>. The exercises under Some Practice With Addressing the Public Audience of Your Media Essay move the students through practical steps and creative exercises for developing an appropriate voice for their own essay.

<u>Arranging</u> <u>the</u> <u>Essay</u>. The writing of this essay will probably occasion some classroom discussion on the nature of "media researcher," as the primary role of the writer for this task is designated. It combines elements of the expository as well as the critical and argumentative. The writer must be able to derive some sense of theme in the media materials under examination, and then arrange these materials so that a generalization can be derived. This is a substantial task in itself, but we feel that the careful reading of the professional essays in this chapter and a discussion of the model student essay should result in some interesting work.

Both of the professional essays and the rough draft of the student essay "Horrors" are worth discussing for what they illustrate about how students might arrange their essay by moving back and forth between generalization and specification. You might ask students to update McDermott's list of teenage films and then generalize about the attitudes of the films toward teenagers. If this generalization conflicts with McDermott's, as a class they can then form a new generalization about teenage films in the 1980s and early 1990s. Then, they can revise the essay, substituting their new generalization and adding a paragraph or two that discusses the films they have listed and the generalization they have developed about them.

Grossberger's essay combines the aims of exploration and explanation as he searches for the cause of "Wheel of Fortune's" phenomenal popularity; his exploration leads him through considerable research as he amasses details in support of his final generalization. Students will be interested to see how each new set of data lead him to a new generalization, which he then discards.

In discussing "Horrors," you can ask your students to point out where the writer might have strengthened the essay by developing his shaping idea (horror films are a reflection of 20th-century morals, values, and fears) more thoroughly and clearly throughout the body of the paper. The writer's peers in evaluating his essay felt he didn't generalize clearly enough about how each era of horror films mirrored society, and you will no doubt find your students making the same comment.

Some discussion also of the lack of any clearly named sources of information in the rough draft of "Horrors" might be in order, while you can note that in the final draft, some revisions have been made in order to clarify both the development of the shaping idea and the sources of information.

Does the author of "Horrors" explain the horror genre so as to help his audience see its value and relevance to them? This question can be a bridge between a discussion of how the student generated ideas for his essay and how well he addressed his audience.

Focus on Style: The Components of Style

The matters of style taken up in this section are relevant to an understanding of the stylistic characteristics of a public voice. There is evidence to indicate, for example, that although college teachers often counsel their students to adopt a plain, concrete style of verbal sentence structures, they just as often give higher grades to students who write effectively in the more complex, abstract style of nominal sentences (see Rosemary L. Hake and Joseph Williams, "Style and Its Consequences: Do As I Do, Not As I Say." College English 43 (Sept. 1981): 433-451). Giving students some practice in distinguishing between verbal and nominal sentence structures seems appropriate here. You may even want to suggest to your students that they try to nominalize those sentences throughout the essay they are writing for the Chapter 7 task that develop abstract generalizations, while they focus on offering their concrete examples in a plainer, verbal style.

The information that follows on balanced phrasing, loose and periodic sentences, and figurative language introduces students to those elements of style that draw a reader's attention from the content to the richness of the language used to express that content. This section, along with the Focus section in Chapter 8, can be used to help students clarify their ideas by employing, for example, a figure of speech to make an abstraction more concrete; it also can be used to direct students' attention to the emotional and aesthetic qualities of language, hopefully making them more sensitive to style when they read as well as when they write.

The exercises in Some Practice with Style are intended, first, to help students understand more concretely the nature of nominal, verbal, loose, periodic, active, and passive constructions (Exercises 1-3); second, to give students practice in these matters by revising a passage from Thoreau to make it more concrete, and another from White to make it more abstract (Exercises 4 and 5); third, to have students analyze both sentence structure and the use of figurative language in two passages by White (Exercise 6); and fourth, to have students apply what they have learned by making a passage from their own writing more abstract, then more concrete, then more eloquent (Exercises 7-9).

The sentences in the first three exercises might be recast as follows:
1.   a. Your taking the high road and my taking the low road will get me to Scotland before you (verbal to nominal).
       b. Many people today are preoccupied with physical fitness (nominal to verbal).
       c. Because of television, we don't wonder at the news anymore (nominal to verbal).
       d. Attempting to inflict my young thoughts and experiences on others by putting them on paper, something I worked at even as a child, shows my continuing appreciation for the essay (verbal to nominal).

2.   a. The animal survived, having a thick coat of fur (periodic to loose).
       b. Our hero saved the day, mercilessly goading the bully (periodic to loose).
       c. Even as they give countless children hours of gleeful play, snowstorms make driving hazardous and thus endanger lives (loose to periodic).
       d. Offering an artful combination of news, popular opinion, and gossip, newspapers are popular (loose to periodic).

3.   a. Government policy, paradoxically, often worries and frustrates members of a free society (passive to active).
       b. The swirling winds of the tornado tore the house apart (passive to active).
       c. He was tired out by the hard day's work at the factory (active to passive).
       d. Before they hatch, your chickens should not be counted by you (active to passive).

Note also that in discussing the passages by White in Exercise 6, in the first passage you might point our White's use of a nominal structure in sentence 2, his predominant emphasis throughout the rest of the passage on active, verbal sentences, and his use of a simile in sentence 4, personification in sentence 6, and a metaphor in sentence 9; in the second passage, you might focus discussion on his use of an extended metaphor, of balanced phrasing in sentences 2, 4, 6, 7, and 8, and of a simile in sentence 9.

Rewriting

In going over this section with your students, you might want to concentrate on reviewing the style of the revised version of "Horrors." For example, might the student writer have clarified

58

his paper further by nominalizing the sentences in the third paragraph? Have your class compare the third paragraph with the seventh in this respect. You might also discuss with them how nominalization might have helped clarify the purpose of the essay at the start and/or how the writer did use modifying strings of adjectives and adverbs or clusters of subordinate clauses to convey his abstract ideas in paragraphs 3, 5, 6, 7, 8, and 11.

Conversely, how effective is the writer in conveying concrete information in a plain, verbal style? One problem the peer readers had with the rough draft of the essay was the way in which it overwhelmed them with information. You might hold a class discussion on how the author of "Horrors" might have consolidated his information more thoroughly than he managed to do even in his final draft, by combining the information in paragraphs 4 and 5, for example, or in paragraphs 9 and 10.

Becoming Aware of Yourself as a Writer

These questions in Chapter 7 are intended to prompt students to review for themselves the elements of explanation they have been introduced to. The importance of gathering information from other sources is emphasized in questions 1 and 2. The role played by generalization is reviewed in questions 3 and 5. Question 4 asks students to generalize about the characteristics of a public voice, while question 6 asks them to generalize about the difference between their personal, private voice and the public voice they employed in order to explain effectively.

CHAPTER EIGHT: WRITING ABOUT AN ISSUE--ARGUING YOUR POINT OF
                 VIEW

     This and the following chapter focus on arguing an issue.
Chapter 8 emphasizes the strategies and formal logical components
of argument; Chapter 9 the importance of critical thinking in
arriving at a possible resolution of a controversial issue. A
knowledge of argument--its methodologies, pitfalls, rhetorical
devices--seems more and more crucial to many educators in the
'90's. As Kinneavy's third aim in writing after the expressive
and the referential or expository, it is gaining prominence in
many classrooms where argumentative and persuasive discourse seems
increasingly to academics to be inherent in the language and
procedures of other disciplines.

     The triangle diagram has been used by many rhetoricians to
point out, first, the complexities of the writing process and,
second, the manner in which the various components relate to each
other. While reader, writer, subject, and text are all present in
any writing situation, the writer stresses a different component
depending upon his or her aim in writing. The expressive aim
focuses on the writer; the expository, on the subject; the
persuasive, on the reader; and the literary on the text itself.

     Students have, of course, been involved in argumentation all
of their lives, in both its bold and subtle forms. In both their
personal and public lives, they have felt the pull of persuasion,
and they have asserted their viewpoints as well. That they may
not often win an argument may be a motivation for learning how an
effective argument is constructed.

     They have no doubt been asked to write an argument in some
course or another. Whether they have ever been introduced to logic
and to more formal methods of organizing an argument will vary
greatly. For the task in this chapter, we ask students to create
a case in which they, as one of the participants, must argue the
merits of some aspect of the situation, hoping to persuade the
other participants, whether neutral or hostile.

Purpose

     Students are often quite taken with the whole idea of appeals
in argument and of course argument's emphasis on audience--as
indicated by the triangle--brings out the student's contemporary
reality of a world of competing discourses much more vividly than
any other writing task. The worlds of politics and entertainment
provide inexhaustible material for an introductory lesson on
argument, ranging from the individual styles of politicians like
President Bush and Senator Kennedy to entertainment icons like

Mick Jagger and Madonna.

Although students are fascinated by argument, they are also repelled by what they construe as manipulation and exploitation. You might want to discuss the limits of persuasion in a democratic society and consider how binding is the ethical appeal in the media and government. Citing actual examples from the news might give a real immediacy to the working out of a case for this chapter's task.

Task: Arguing Your Point of View on an Issue

We have used a case approach here as a way for the student to generate an issue and see its significance in a context, locate a role, and acquire a vivid sense of audience. Students don't often get this easily; you will probably need to give them some practice in seeing the components of a case. Examples from the daily newspaper should help, as well as other cases you and your students can devise. You might also begin with a well-known controversial public figure in politics, entertainment, or sports and build a case around this person.

You may also wish to have each group develop a case among them, so that they share an issue in common and each takes the role of a different participant in the situation. The issue chosen should be one that all group members have differing viewpoints on so that no two students are arguing from the same point of view. In this way, each writer acquires a variety of neutral and hostile readers.

Writing Your Essay

Generating Ideas: We have tried to discuss the major argumentative strategies and methods in this chapter but you don't have to cover all the material in this section in order to establish a workable case on an issue. Stephen Toulmin's strategies for making claims while taking into account the need to consider warrants and qualifiers are particularly useful for showing students the logic of argument. They can suggest some relevant classroom discussion on the social and cultural assumptions that form the contextual background of many of our strongly held values and beliefs, as well as point students toward the selection and evaluation of evidence for their arguments.

The brief arguments by Clark, Thurow, and Kreisberg--all of which originally appeared as New York Times Op-Ed articles--offer interesting starting points for discussing claims and evidence. Students can create cases out of these or other situations suggested by the writers. Each peer group can develop fuller arguments on the issues involved and present them as cases to the entire class.

The excerpts from essays by Sagan, Hofstadter and Freiberg are useful inductive models and also illustrate more fully how claims need to be considered in terms of evidence and qualifiers.

In the passage from The Dragons of Eden, Carl Sagan presents a hypothesis, rather than a conclusion, about "the long-term significance of teaching language to other primates" than the chimpanzee, which, as he goes to some pains to inform us, has learned 10 percent of the words considered Basic English. By presenting this one example of animal ability to think abstractly, Sagan strongly suggests that if all animals were taught language, they would develop abstract thought. While the example of one animal's language acquisition does not represent a random sampling of all animals--in fact, if may be an atypical example--still it is so striking an example that it advances the argument considerably. Students may not agree, of course, for a number of reasons: one, the chimp's intelligence has been presented to us over a long-enough period that we are will willing to accept his intelligence without ascribing the same abilities to other animals; two, the thought that man and animals are on the same intelligence scale is threatening for both religious reasons and for reasons of our historical sense of human superiority. In order to place Sagan's method in a different context so that students can analyze it objectively, you might want to present them with an analogous situation: if life were discovered on Mars, how would that one discovery affect the argument that there is life on other planets and throughout the solar system?

Richard Hofstadter's essay on Abraham Lincoln advances by analogy its argument that Lincoln freed the slaves only as a last resort: "The Emancipation Proclamation of January 1, 1863, had all the moral grandeur of a bill of lading." He then proceeds to list the ignoble aspects of the Proclamation. He does not sustain the analogy to a logical conclusion, however, because he concedes that "For all its limitations, the Emancipation Proclamation probably made genuine emancipation inevitable."

Selma Fraiberg's passage from The Magic Years is an example of causal generalization. Her argument is that "the real threat to humanity does not lie in neurosis but in the diseases of the ego, the diseases of isolation, detachment and emotional sterility." By presenting the causes of a healthy, even a neurotic human being, Fraiberg explains the causes of "the hollow man."

Ellen Goodman makes the claim that the "series of exclamation point books all concerned with How to Make It" are urging us to be unethical. Students may argue that by giving only one example--

that of Michael Korda's Success!-- Goodman is not presenting a random sampling of all such books. However, they will see that she presents a fair sampling of ways in which Korda "eliminates value judgments and edits out moral questions."

For another example of the use of a string of syllogisms in a primarily deductive argument, you might refer your students at this point to Martin Luther King's "Letter from a Birmingham Jail."

The assumptions on which the 10 enthymemes in "Some Practice With Deduction" are based are the following:

1. Any major that offers job opportunities is good.
2. Anything that affects our health is a vital issue.
3. Anything that the middle class cannot afford should be subsidized by the government.
4. Anything that encourages mind-body coordination should be encouraged.
5. Americans should train or retrain in any field that offers high employment.
6. Anything that causes a disease is harmful.
7. No system of education that does not teach English well should be encouraged.
8. Anything that makes people feel good should not be considered worthless.
9. Anything that repudiates the philosophy of the women's movement should itself be repudiated.

Arguments 4 and 8 can be considered red herrings since the main issues aroused by video games and advertising are being ignored--that video games consume too much of children's time and money and that advertising is often unscrupulous in its claims. Argument 6 may be considered to be ascribing a false cause since the sexual revolution itself did not cause disease; at best it is a secondary cause.

The fallacies in assumptions a-j under Some Practice With Identifying Deductive Fallacies are as follows:

a. Genetic fallacy
b. Red herring
c. Bandwagon
d. Ad hominem
e. Ad hominem
f. Either/or
g. Begging the question
h. False cause
i. Genetic fallacy
j. False analogy

In "Some Practice With the Classical Questions as Means of Generating Ideas for an Argument," the shaping idea "Natural foods are healthier than processed ones" can be developed by the classical questions "What is it?", "What are the differences between?", "What are the effect?", "What caused this?", and "What examples are there?"

"Dogs are better pets than cats" can be developed by "What are the similarities and differences?", "What are the reasons for this?" and "What are the effects?"

"Cocaine is America's Number One social problem" lends itself to such questions as "What examples are there of it?", "What are the causes and effects of it?", "How does it compare and contrast?", and "What analogy is useful?"

"America should adopt more vigorous measures for feeding the hungry people of the world" might be proven through "What is it?", "What examples are there?", and "Why should this be done?"

Audience: Persuading Your Audience

In "Some Practice With Persuading Your Audience," Lewis Thomas established his credibility with his audience through his obvious knowledge of biology: the terminology he used and the processes he explained. Most readers of his book would be informed by the publisher that his is a doctor.

Thomas was not playing the role of a doctor, but of an informed, thoughtful human being, essentially a peer of the reader, whom he assumed to be educated, open-minded, and concerned also. Correspondingly, he adopted an informal but serious and human tone, alternately trusting, fair, or in need of consolation. Because he wrote for an educated reader, he assumed some biological background and so gave considerable depth, not as a biologist but as an informed citizen--he does define his words and explain his concepts, however.

He was, of course, aware that his readers may cling to the notion that man is superior to the rest of life, but because he assumed his reader is open-minded, he gently led the reader through his discoveries about the complexity of life, thereby reinforcing, if not creating, the open-minded attitude he assumed.

He used similes (Paragraphs 1, 4, 5, 10), personification (5-7), and metaphor (7, 10). In the last paragraph, he used the analogy that the entire earth is like a cell; in so doing, he attempted to alter the way in which we think about biological life: it is not hierarchical nor is it like an organism with orderly processes performed by discrete parts; rather, it is a series of isolated, at times anarchic, systems.

Arranging Your Essay

Arguing an issue requires a clearly stated and limited shaping idea. This is also a good time to discuss the nature and validity of evidence that students intend to use in their drafts. They might discuss their use of evidence within their peer groups and also get some comment on the effectiveness and scope of their claims. Some students have rather sweeping claims and thus make some excessively broad proposals on these claims.

You might want to review the different parts of an argument before students begin their drafts. Ask some students how they intend to open their arguments; you may want to suggest some dramatic or rhetorically rousing introductions for their cases, even posing alternative openings if applicable.

If students are working in groups, they might exchange the frames of reference of their own roles for those of their group members so that each writer knows the frame of reference of his audience. Students might also want to exchange outlines of their arguments in order to prepare successful refutations.

The assumptions of the framers of "The Declaration of Independence" that all men are created equal and have unalienable rights that they can defend against unjust governments are invalid only if the injured state seeks change "for light and transient causes." The argument rests on this syllogism: All people may abolish governments that destroy their rights/Britain had destroyed Americans' rights/Therefore, British rule should be abolished.

The Declaration has four parts to its argument: Statement of argument (Paragraphs 1 and 2); refutation (Paragraph 2 and second paragraph from end); proof (all the paragraphs beginning "He has" or "For..."); and conclusion (last paragraph).

The arguments of the opposition are that the United States should negotiate longer with Great Britain and that "Governments long established should not be changed for light and transient causes," but the framers of the Declaration assert a higher authority in that the rule of a despotic government should be thrown off.

The evidence presented seems quite exhaustive and both informs the audience and proves the argument.

As Representatives of the various states, the writers gain credibility in presenting their case. Their voice is that of aggrieved, determined, responsible citizens.

The audience was varied--supportive, neutral, and hostile. Americans themselves were divided between those that supported the Declaration and those who did not; the Declaration would rally those who supported the break with Britain and those who had previously been neutral as well as inform other countries. It would anger the British and their American allies. The writers were cordial but firm; their tone, knowledgeable, solemn, and determined. Because of their dedication to their cause and their thoroughness in supporting it, their cause seems just.

"Rachel McLish," on the other hand, wanted to redefine bodybuilding and advocate it for women. Her assumption was that "A woman bodybuilder does not lose any of her femininity, she gains sexuality." For proof, she offers her four-point plan which seems ultimately reasonable; her arrangement pattern is cause nd effect. Her opponents' point of view is that bodybuilding leads to masculine looking women; she denies that this is the case. She informs her readers who, she assumes, do not know much about her subject but are open-minded; the readers of more traditional magazines might be more hostile, and she would have to go to greater lengths to reassure them, perhaps also minimize the gain in sexuality. Cosmopolitan subscribers, on the other hand, would need even less convincing and could absorb more depth. Her voice is that of a knowledgeable female bodybuilder who sincerely and earnestly wishes to spread the good word.

Focus: Persuasive Language and the Appeal to the Emotions

The logical components of King's argument are primarily deductive; in fact, he employs a string of syllogisms, appealing to higher priorities to counter his opponents' claim that his actions lead to violent extremism.

Para. 1.   All who do not support non-violence are stumbling
           blocks.
           White moderates do not support non-violence.
           White moderates are stumbling blocks.

Para. 2   All societies with law and order should establish
           justice.
           The South is a society with law and order.
           The South should establish justice.

Para. 3   All men must try to gain their constitutional rights.
           Negroes are men.
           Negroes must try to gain their constitutional rights.

           Those fighting for their civil rights are not

responsible for the violence caused by those who would deny them their rights.
The Negroes are fighting for their constitutional rights.
They are not responsible for violence caused by their opponents.

Para. 4   All people who would do good must use time wisely.
           Negroes would do good.
           They must use time wisely.

Para. 5   All that is extreme is at either end of a continuum.
  & 6   Non-violence is not at either end of a continuum.
           Non-violence is not extreme.

Para. 7   If non-violence is not supported, then a violent extreme will take over.
           The Negroes' non-violent movement is not supported.
           The violent faction (Muslims) will take over.

Para. 8   All oppressed people cannot remain oppressed forever.
           The Negroes are oppressed.
           They cannot remain oppressed forever.

Para. 9   Inductive argument by analogy.

Para.10   All who would root out injustice must take strong, persistent, determined action.
           The Negroes must root out injustice.
           They must take strong, persistent, determined action.

King's attitude toward his audience was one of disappointment and anger. His tone was one of chastisement. ("I have been gravely disappointed with the white moderate.")

He juxtaposes words with negative and positive connotations to indicate the obnoxious quality that peace can sometimes have and the creative element that extremism can generate. He also uses many words and figures of speech with religious connotations to appeal to his audience of white ministers. He uses some clichés because they are familiar and have a safe connotation for his reader. He also uses words like "law and order" and "justice" to underscore the rationality of his course. If he had been writing to a group of senators, rather than ministers, his language would have been even more rational and not religious.

The framers of the Declaration of Independence used much more rational language than did King; even their terminology for God is couched in more rational terms ("Supreme Judge of the World").

Correspondingly, they used fewer figures of speech and words with little connotative power. Theirs was a political document, King's an ethical, even religious one.

Rewriting

"Rachel McLish" has substituted, added, rearranged, consolidated and distributed in revising her essay on bodybuilding. In Paragraph 1, she added the categorical statement: "Bodybuilding has become more than a sport--it has become a way of life." She has added paragraph 2 in answer to her readers' request for information about how her subject related to the women's movement. In paragraph 3, she has added more technical information on the reasons for and results of bodybuilding, perhaps in answer to her readers' request for reassurance that they would not become muscular.

She has also rearranged sentences in paragraph 3 since the emphatic last sentence originally was buried in the middle. Paragraph 6 has been consolidated (it was once four paragraphs), rearranged while being consolidated, and the chair analogy distributed (it originally appeared only in the conclusion).

The paragraph that appeared just before the conclusion has also been omitted, perhaps because it did not fit smoothly into the original outline. Your students might consider what else she might have done with this material.

Finally, she added a last sentence that strengthened her conclusion.

In responding to the "Audience Response Guide," students should consider what issue the writer is concerned with and what position he or she is taking on the issue (question 1); how successfully the writer has appealed to the intended reader logically, emotionally, and ethically (both questions 2 and 3 since audience appeal is the primary aim of this task); and how these appeals can be strengthened (question 4).

In evaluating the essay for this task, you will probably want to give primary consideration to the students' handling of the three appeals although, since juggling all three is a difficult task, you may want to give primary consideration to the logical and ethical and secondary consideration to the use of language.

Becoming Aware of Yourself as a Writer

These questions might form the basis of a class discussion in preparation for the next task in which students will be asked to think critically about several well-known arguments on national issues.

CHAPTER NINE: WRITING ABOUT AN ISSUE--JOINING A DEBATE

This chapter continues the previous chapter's emphasis on argument but focuses on the process of critical thinking--the self-examination and self-appraisal of our discursive practices-- to provide students with an introduction to higher-order thinking on issues of national importance, issues that are so controversial because they implicate some of our society's bedrock attitudes on life, death and sexual morality.

The crucial nature of these issues requires a discourse that can convey ideas maturely, i.e. objectively and rationally, to an audience of informed, literate readers. It isn't coincidental that in a rhetoric text these ideas are conveyed largely by academics, or at least professionals who write in a scholarly way. We recognize the compelling urge of academic writers to address a like-minded "discourse community" in an acceptable, cogent style. And the desire of college teachers to introduce their students to this language of the academy. The advantage of critical thinking is that we can examine why this is so, and how this tendency influences the way we argue these issues.

In fulfilling the task for this chapter, we believe you and your students can examine--through the model essays and explanatory material--what the purpose and scope of serious discourse in a college community can reasonably accomplish in its attempt to educate students in a democratic society.

We are asking students to understand that most issues are complex, with varying, perhaps equally legitimate points of view, and with many ramifications for society. We ask them to both learn and understand the varying points of view and to synthesize them in the attempt to resolve the conflict or at least to encourage the dialogue to continue in a new way. The student writer is to play the role of disinterested observer writing for an informed reader, reaching a broader viewpoint or resolution that in some small way is original.

Purpose

We introduce students to the concept of critical thinking at the same time that we inform them that they have been urged to practice these skills throughout their education, particularly in essay examinations. You may wish to ask students their definitions of critical thinking prior to reading the chapter in an inductive approach to the concepts involved. You may also wish to examine the questions on randomly chosen essay exams for examples of questions calling for critical thinking--and for examples of those that do not.

By now, students should recognize that thinking and writing involve chains of generalizations, but you might want to make reference to the tasks in earlier chapters as reinforcement.

Task: Joining a Debate on an Issue

We have chosen three issues that touch almost everyone in our society: abortion, euthanasia, and pornography. We have selected essays that we thought would ground students in the significant positions and terms of debate for each issue. They certainly are not definitive as arguments for or against these issues, and you may want to supplement the essays with any relevant materials you may choose. You may also want to use more passionately or eloquently expressed pleas on both sides for comparison.

The student must be able to read critically for this task as well as write critically. We have included a set of questions after each group of essays on an issue to assist students in grappling with each essay and its contribution to the debate. Additional questions in the Task section assist them in determining how each essay they read helps them in their critical thinking about the issue. We suggest answers to the questions following each group of essays at the end of this Task section.

The task lends itself to a collaborative approach. You might, for example, divide the class into groups and have each group choose an issue. Each member of the group can research a major point of view for them. Once each point of view has been researched and role-played, all group members can then form their own resolution of the issue.

Questions on Abortion:

1. Van Den Haag seeks a middle position for the continuing conflict between religious and secular claims about abortion. Petchesky discusses a broad range of social issues centering on women's rights, particularly the rights of minority women. Garvey, writing in a religious journal of opinion, takes a narrower point of view and is concerned with how to make pro-life a more persuasive point of view. Of the three, Petchesky seems least concerned about the moral dimensions of the issue, focusing on what she refers to as "social rights."
2. By arguing for early abortion or the use of abortifacient pills, Van Den Haag seems to favor pro-choice, but he also doesn't deny that there are rational arguments for making abortion unconstitutional.
3. Petchesky uses personal experience, statistics, expert testimony and social and historical analysis.
4. Petchesky grounds women's rights in choice; Garvey does not see choice as a given human right.

5. Both Van Den Haag and Petchesky recognize the importance of Roe v. Wade for the future of abortion choice. Van Den Haag suggests it could be revoked; Petchesky would certainly be against it; Garvey does not mention Roe v. Wade but would probably be against it.
6. Open to discussion.

Questions on Euthanasia:

1. Rachels needs to provide a theoretical basis for rejecting passive in favor of active euthanasia. Johnson uses the important Cruzan case for establishing her view that the choice of euthanasia resides with the family, not the state.
2. Hunter would not deny the dying person the experience of the "spiritual, emotional, and historical meaning of death." Active euthanasia would prevent this.
3. Literary and philosophical allusions and quotations present the reader with a larger dimension and insight into the subject. They carry the weight of inherited wisdom, forming a kind of timeless evidence.
4. Rachels feels that passive euthanasia is actually unethical and in some cases even cruel. Physicians must consider the moral consequences of their professional ethics. Concern for the individual patient's unique situation might be a way to resolve the conflict between active and passive euthanasia.
5. Physicians must consider the moral and ethical nature of their professional acts. Physicians have taken an oath to protect life. Physicians are more frequently called on to make life or death decisions.
6. Many students have had some personal experience with terminal illness and euthanasia. This most certainly will affect their position on this issue.

Questions on Pornography:

1. Steinem is against the imbalance of power between men and women which results in sex as aggression against women. She gives many examples of contemporary pornography, relates language to cultural practices, and provides a theoretical distinction between the erotic and the pornographic. Sheinfeld considers any departure from free speech as ill-advised. Government censorship can actually be used against women, and no direct cause has been determined between pornography and violence. Miller asserts that the prohibition of "sexual subordination" does not constitute censorship; freedom of speech, in any event, is not an absolute right, and pornography results in real acts of violence toward women.
2. Open to discussion.
3. Sheinfeld and Miller mainly restrict themselves to the legal and procedural implications of government legislation.

Steinem, writing for a broader audience, ranges widely and
sees pornography as having wide social and cultural
ramifications.
4. Personal examples give support and credibility to
generalizations on pornography. They provide evidence for the
actual impact of sexually explicit materials on society.
5. Offer analogies with other areas of constitutional conflict,
e.g. civil rights or debate on war powers. Individual cases
may or may not point to an inevitable loss of free speech.
6. Steinem's purpose differs from the other writers. Because she
is approaching the subject of pornography as part of a large
view of human sexual expressiveness, she draws on a variety of
evidence for her argument, much of it from popular culture.

Generating Ideas: Critical Thinking

We have isolated four aspects of critical thinking as a way
of simplifying a complex series of skills and enabling students to
master an approach to thinking critically. The four skills are
applied to two issues here: abortion and whether the college
curriculum should emphasize the liberal arts or technologies.
Suggestions are made as to how students can best "get inside" an
issue: The first is the use of the journal for summarizing
opposing points of view and then freewriting about one's own
encounters with the issue and also for writing dialogues between
or among characters representing the major points of view on an
issue. Another suggestion for understanding all points of view is
collaboration with a group of other students, each of whom might
be asked to play the role of one of the major points of view on
an issue.

The exercises ask students to experiment with these methods:
to write dialogues, to role-play in a group, to write summaries in
their journals. Question 2 asks them to analyze the media's
treatment of a controversial issue to determine how objective the
viewpoint is. Question 4 asks students to list issues they think
cannot be resolved and to indicate their characteristics; you may
be able to intervene here and indicate how a resolution might
indeed be reached.

We draw attention here also to the importance of evaluating
evidence in argument. Making students aware of the broad range of
allusions in the professional essays will help them to become more
aware of the importance of taking a broad outlook on an issue, and
to be more cautious about their own personal bias in making
conclusions about controversial issues.

Audience: The Informed Reader

We are asking the student to perform a typical, but always difficult task--that of writing for an informed reader, probably you, the teacher. The question is what can a student say to a teacher that can make a contribution to the teacher's understanding of the subject? We suggest here that students use role-play as a means of getting inside an issue and understanding the varying viewpoints in order to produce an honest response that may contribute to the reader's appreciation of the issue. The exercises here encourage students to role-play the major players in familiar controversies.

By role-playing all the viewpoints, the writer also is able to think critically and objectively as he or she must for an informed reader. We also remind students that informed readers do not need much background on the subject and that they expect the writer to write well, observing the conventions.

Arranging the Essay

Once the student has chosen an issue, has read the background literature, has role-played, summarized, and collaborated, he or she may still be in a quandary as to how to arrive at a broader point of view and how to organize the paper. Organizing the paper may in fact prove to be an important heuristic for arriving at a synthesis. We suggest students use the four questions for developing critical thinking skills as an outline for the essay, using the order in which we present them. This order enables students to engage in "syllogistic" reasoning: if it is true that (first point of view on the issue), and if it is true that (second point of view, etc.), then, given all the ramifications and related issues, this conclusion must result.

We have included a brief analysis of one of the professional essays to show students how they might consider organizing their own contribution to the debate on an issue.

They should also read the student essay both in its rough and final forms before writing their first draft because the writer fell into the understandable pitfall in writing her rough draft of submerging her synthesis in an argument for one point of view. Her final draft, in which she presents different points of view and emphasizes her synthesis independently of either side, becomes a good example of critical thinking. Students should also see that, while she does not resolve the issue, she offers an interesting new angle on it that could change the focus of the debate.

Focus on the Writer: Joining the Community of Discourse

Rather than focusing on another constituent of style or form, we chose to introduce students to the governing contextual circle in which, as student writers, they derive their ideas as to how to present their writing to an audience of academic readers and writers. There is much discussion currently in writing journals about "discourse communities" and their effect either beneficial or baleful on student writers.

You might consider this section an amplification of much of what we have said earlier in the text on audience, but with the added realization that our very way of conceiving a subject and defining it is done in terms of where we stand within a specialized, rarefied world of readers and writers. You might want to elicit from students other forceful discursive models, such as rap and rock lyrics and performing styles adapted to a critical audience, or medical evaluations of ethical issues directed to an audience of physicians.

The exercises asks students to interpret the conventions and strategies of discourse communities they are familiar with and some with which they are not, such as middlebrow journals of opinion like Harper's and Atlantic. You may want to take a kind of census of the various discourse communities in which students claim or disclaim participation.

Rewriting

As we indicated above, the student has revised her rough draft considerably, changing it from an essentially one-sided essay to one that thinks critically about the issue and offers a new generalization in synthesis of the opposing points of view. To do so, she had to add material that explains the case for pornography and recognizes the legitimacy of the free speech defense. She also shows the ramifications of the feminist/fundamentalist collaboration on the issue. Her conclusion attempts to reinforce her synthesis, located in paragraph 5, but it could restate it yet more clearly and forcefully. She has not adequately heeded Quintillian's advice about stating the synthesis firmly at the end.

The questions on rewriting and editing to sharpen critical thinking should provide a self-help list or a framework for further peer and teacher evaluation.

Becoming Aware of Yourself as a Writer

These questions might form the basis for an interesting class discussion as well as for a student/teacher conference or for journal entries.

CHAPTER TEN: WRITING ABOUT RESEARCH--TESTING A HYPOTHESIS

     The research or investigative paper is in many composition
classes the culminating writing activity of the term.   In some
colleges, writing classes function in a service capacity, mainly
enabling students to acquire the conventions of academic discourse
that are demanded in research for the social sciences, the
sciences, the technologies, and the humanities.   It is assumed
that the English class will provide all the necessary instruction
and practice to ensure mastery of essential research skills like
note-taking, outlining, critical thinking, source interpretation,
the conventions of documentation and scholarship.   In reality, of
course, the results are often quite less than encouraging.
Instructors cringe at the prospect of plowing through yet another
set of dull, fact-laden, ill-examined investigations.   Plagiarism
wafts threateningly through the room. Research papers often seem
to yield far fewer profitable results than they should.

     Part of the problem may lie in the assignment itself.   An
instructor who sends a class out to complete a twenty-page paper
can expect little more than a pastiche of linked quotations that
makes little sense to either writer or reader.   The research paper
can be a very valuable assignment, one that will carry over across
the curriculum to prepare students for investigative work in other
disciplines.   But the assignment must be a reasonable one, and it
must provide activities that do more than ask for the accumulation
of fact.

     Because we stress throughout Way to Writing that students can
acquire writing skills by using what they already know combined
with inventive strategies that take them further into a subject,
we feel that by the time students are assigned the research paper,
they will not find it such a strange, impenetrable task.   They
have, in effect, been doing research all along.   In the course of
fulfilling the previous chapter tasks, they staked out a subject,
acquired data, interpreted and criticized possible arrangements
for this material, and addressed their findings to a specific
audience. Writing the paper for this chapter task, then, makes use
of these already acquired skills but directs them to deeper and
more complex expository demands.

     The nature of the assignment requires that students be given
ample time to undertake the steps involved in moving through the
stages of library research.   You may want to introduce the chapter
purpose and task several weeks before you anticipate the due date
for the paper.   We like to sketch the assignment out briefly in
class two weeks before we actively pursue the problems involved.
We talk about possible topics, suggesting that they might
incorporate assignments being given in their other classes.   We

also try to arrange that students have at least a week, preferably two, to revise rough drafts and hand in the final draft. We also try to arrange with the college library staff a planned research session that will direct students to materials, give them practice in using the library facilities, and give you the chance to offer them on-the-spot advice about specific research problems they might encounter. We have found this library session helpful in giving us some input into the actual process of their investigations.

We provide in this chapter a concise but usable guide to the stages of research. We stress the techniques of arrangement that traditionally constitute the conventions of research, emphasizing to students how efficient use of these conventions can help get them through their task. The exercises direct them to decisions they will encounter in the course of their investigations.

Purpose

We begin with an example of induction in order to introduce to students what will be the principle of both invention and arrangement for the task. We explain how this will be used for scientific investigation but also how it applies in other subject areas. Then we pose the need for a particular kind of reader that can digest the data that the writer will gather. Our goal, as we state, is to "create a discourse that has the authority of skillful, objective research." You might want to spend some time surveying the scientific interest or lack of it in your class. Most students, even the least scientifically sophisticated among them, welcome the opportunity to pursue investigations that fall outside the curriculum of basic introductory science and social science courses. At this point, we outline the procedures we expect them to follow and respond to any question they might have about the intended audience for this task.

Task: Writing About Research

We have chosen to make this a "writing across the curriculum" task by recommending that students research and test a hypothesis related to the natural or social sciences. By asking them to form a hypothesis based on their own observations in one of these areas, we have sought to ground the assignment firmly in their own experience in order to help insure that they want to know the answer to the research question. By combining the social and natural sciences as a field for research, we think we have given students a sufficiently broad expanse of subject matter from which to cull possible observations of vital interest to them.

We ask students to form a hypothesis and attempt to prove or disprove it in order to encourage them to understand the scientific method. Of course, it would be unrealistic to suppose that a freshman research essay would perform the same functions as a working scientist's investigation and creation of original knowledge, but we stress to our students that their synthesis of others' findings on a specific subject and their own observations is a form of knowledge that makes a contribution to their audience's view of that subject; a reader will profit from the unique arrangement they have created. This is particularly true when the student's hypothesis, formulated as it is on lay knowledge of a subject, is shared by any number of people.

You may want to spend some time discussing just what objective research is and what kinds of choices among sources students might face. Unless they have had some experience in writing research papers in high school, their idea of research is largely a collection of whatever information they could get their hands on, not much different from a grade school child's "report." We review with our students the kind of writing and thinking they employed in completing their previous tasks in order to show them how those activities were really kinds of research.

We set out a recommended length for this paper, but we have ourselves varied the length of the assignment with our own classes. Five to eight pages is sufficient to give students experience in gathering a substantial number of sources, interpreting and evaluating the relative usefulness of those sources for their subject, and then arranging and documenting their material for an audience familiar with the conventions of research.

Generating Ideas Through Induction

We explain induction as a fundamental process of perception; therefore, the examples we cite are drawn from everyday experience. Through our discussion of the process, we draw attention to some of the fallacies that result from faulty induction. You may want to offer examples of your own to show how our perceptual process can lead us astray.

The passage from Polanyi's book can lead to a more general discussion of how our point of view can distort the evidence we cite and the conclusions we draw.

Surely one of the most daunting of tasks for students undertaking any form of research among printed sources is the need to choose sources they can use and have confidence in from among all the possible sources they might encounter. You might supplement our discussion on evaluating sources by bringing into class books and periodicals from the library in order to elicit evaluative comments from the class. You might also ask students to show their tentative bibliography to their peer groups and ask them to evaluate these sources. You might also ask peer groups to conduct mock interviews of "authorities" on a variety of topics to give them practice in setting up questions and surveys.

The exercises in Some Practice with Induction and Evaluating Sources give additional activities for understanding how inductive thinking pervades our mental responses. Exercise 1 asks students to consider the possibility of total objectivity, the kind we often associate with the camera. Exercise 2 asks them to role-play the task of the anthropologist, who must gather information without imposing his own values or expectations. We ask students to be as innocent and naive as possible about rituals they themselves have been born into. Exercise 3 can be a profitable group project and can lead to research topics other than those suggested later in this chapter. Exercise 4 illustrates some of the causes of faulty inductive thinking: a. hasty generalization; b. inadequate number of examples; c. unreliable source. Exercise 5 asks them to evaluate library sources in a specific subject area. This can be a preliminary exercise for investigating their own hypothesis. Exercise 6 asks them to evaluate the objectivity of a variety of sources.

We suggest the use of a personal research journal as a way to answer some of the questions that arise while pursuing a research assignment. The exercises that follow suggest specific ways the journal might be used in the beginning stages of their research.

Addressing Your Audience: The Lay Reader

This chapter section would not have had much to say a few years ago. Scientific writing for the informed but technically uneducated reader did not really exist. At one end of the spectrum were the essentially how-to-do-it magazines like Popular Mechanics; at the other end was the fascinating but often excessively demanding Scientific American. Recently, many interesting and visually attractive publications have filled this void. They are lively yet solidly researched as well. We want students to be aware of them so that they can imagine an audience of similarly interested readers to whom they can address their own investigations. Television, of course, has probably been the most influential medium in attracting interest in scientific topics. Carl Sagan is certainly better known as a media personality than as an author, but his writing and that of Stephen Jay Gould offer excellent models for scientific discourse that is vivid and attention-getting yet not shallow or patronizing. The passage from Gould's article is an excellent example. You might also offset for students an article from a newspaper science supplement such as

The New York Times publishes every Tuesday. Students seeking material can invariably find some here.

You might ask students to bring to class a popular scientific magazine or one that offers articles on contemporary social problems to discuss with regard to their levels of discourse, intended audience, relative use of technical language and the like.

Doing Research

Framing a hypothesis is a mental activity requiring some practice. Essentially, we encourage our students to begin the process by selecting several medical, environmental, psychological, sociological experiences they have had, such as the illness of a friend, the behavior of a group they are familiar with, a religious cult a family member has joined, a natural phenomenon they observed on a camping trip. We then ask them to draw a tentative conclusion or generalization about the meaning of the observation. Students will have drawn conclusions about these subjects already in the course of living through the experiences that generated them, but they need to formalize that conclusion as a positive (or negative) declarative statement, usually one of cause and/or effect: the effects of AIDS on family members is greater than that of any other fatal disease; punk styles do not reflect political rebellion; religious cults give adherents a new feeling of belonging; acid rain is destroying the trees in the Adirondack Mountains.

From their several possible hypotheses, they then proceed to search for sources, do some preliminary reading, and finally choose the most promising hypothesis as their task. Teacher and peer intervention is important at this early stage to insure students understand the framing of a hypothesis as well as how to go about proving or disproving it. They also should know that there is no onus on them to prove the hypothesis right; they should understand that the process is what is important to the scientist.

Few students will come to you with study and research skills adequate enough for you to assume they already know the techniques of note-taking and source gathering. There doesn't seem to be a substitute for going over this information in class with frequent use of the blackboard to reinforce or illustrate a point from the text. Once they have accumulated a body of sources and notes, have them exchange their material with other members of their group who can quickly survey the material for thoroughness and completeness.

The most puzzling aspect of preparing a research paper for most students is recognizing where the language of their sources begins and ends. Most cases of plagiarism are not intentional but simply the failure of students to understand how and where another author's ideas can become theirs. We find that our most difficult task is to show students the differences among quotation, summary and paraphrase, and to convince them that they must document their sources even though they don't quote directly from them. Of course, this goes to the very heart of the research process: integrating someone else's findings into your account, synthesizing material into a new whole.

We provide more concrete advice about putting the paper together than you are apt to find in most other texts. Because the introduction is so vital in the writer's conveying of a convincing scholarly authenticity and clear purpose, we emphasize what a research essay characteristically announces in its opening paragraphs.

You may wish to spend more time on the outline and how the writer gets from a mass of notes to the outline to the rough draft. At various stages along the way, we recommend collecting students' materials to monitor their progress. You can return them with a check or other symbol and ask them to submit all of these again when they submit their final draft. Needless to say, we are wary of any student who can produce a complete paper without also submitting notes and rough draft. But this situation should not occur for the instructor who has been actively involved throughout the writing process for this task.

In responding to Some Practice with Research Methods, students might paraphrase the paragraph in exercise 1 as follows: "The quickly developing area of investigation has been named psychoneuroimmunology and is at last starting to gain the recognition of today's medical authorities who had criticized or neglected former hypotheses of a connection between mind and the body. Much of the research is being helped financially by parts of the National Institutes of Health. Increasingly, as Dr. Osler pointed out, the psychological responses are being recognized as important elements of the cause and care of most sickness."

The summary of the excerpts from Jane Brody's article in exercise 2 might read as follows: "Scientists have finally begun to understand how a person's mental state can affect his illness. New findings in the study of immunology and neurochemistry reveal that human emotion can substantially influence the health by altering the body's response to disease. For example, emotions can alter whiteblood cell level and affect hormonal operation, factors that can combat illness."

A paraphrase of Brody's excerpt might read: "Almost a hundred years after doctors learned the effect of the mind on the body, scientists are beginning to reveal just how the emotions can influence the stages of illness.

"Helped by recent developments in biochemistry, immunology, and neurochemistry, scientists have found that emotions influence working of the nervous system, hormones and disease-fighting functions, operating by way of the brain to affect human susceptibility to many illnesses.

"Investigations have shown that the emotions can affect the functions of whiteblood cells and cause the operation of adrenal gland hormones and neurotransmitters, in so doing influencing the way the body works."

In exercise 3, the student did not change the original wording adequately in a number of places. When the student prepares his paper, he may not realize that an expression like "By unveiling the mechanisms behind these effects" is a direct quotation from the original source.

While we recommend in the text that a research paper be written in a more objective, impartial manner than previous chapter tasks, the student who wrote the model here uses the first person and is quite informal in her introduction. You might ask students to comment on how her informality affects the impact of her research on the reader.

Focus: Documentation

We have included the new Modern Language Association documentation style, in use in PMLA since May 1982. Many instructors, however, still adhere to the traditional form of footnote citation and separate bibliography, so we provide this form as well. The new MLA style is lucid and logical--it's much easier to read an article without the characteristic up and down nodding of the head as one tries to read both text and notes at the same time. The list of "Works Cited" limits the writer to those sources used in the text. The MLA style actually makes footnotes unnecessary in your students' papers. Needless to say, it has received generally complete acceptance with writers and researchers.

Rewriting

The rough draft in this chapter has been revised in response to the peer analysis. Notice that her peer group recommended the removal of both unnecessarily informal expressions on the one hand and language that was too technical on the other; the students were able to determine what they felt the proper tone should be and probably have established a valuable guideline.

In the Revising and Editing Scientific Writing section, we have reviewed the major points of the chapter and also sought to reinforce the revision strategies presented in earlier chapters.

The primary consideration for evaluating this task is the extent to which the writer has skillfully incorporated research techniques and arranged the paper according to the logic and conventions of research. Secondary considerations might include stylistic appropriateness for its intended audience.

Becoming Aware of Yourself as a Writer

These questions ask students to think about the research process they have just completed. We often ask them to look over these questions during their investigations, for they give them some ideas as to how they should be proceeding. They form a good postlude to what is surely to them a monumental accomplishment.

CHAPTER ELEVEN: WRITING ABOUT A SHORT STORY--INTERPRETING A TEXT

    As our statement for the interpretive aim in the general
notes makes clear, interpretation is a process that includes all
the other writing aims, requiring the writer to respond to a text
by bringing to it an expressiveness derived from personal
experience, a willingness to explore possibly unknown territory--
or familiar terrain seen in a new light--an urge to explain one's
discoveries to others, a persuasiveness that derives from the
writer's close reading to the text and requires the writer to
carefully sift all of the discursive evidence at hand.

    Some instructors believe that a formal study of literary
texts has no place in a freshman writing class; others devote a
semester exclusively to reading and writing about literature. We
placed our interpretive chapter at the end of our text because we
believe it incorporates and integrates all the other writing aims
and skills we discuss in earlier chapters and because it forms a
convenient bridge between the two parts of the typical year of
college composition courses.

    Our emphasis in this chapter is less on the terminology of
introduction to literature textbooks and more on the diversity of
student responses to an individual text in journals, peer group
brainstorming and essays that include a significant expressive
element. We want our students to focus on the text itself, but we
also don't shrink from the reality that most students don't
respond to literature unless they can internalize it by seeing a
poem, story, or play as part of their own evolving psychic and
emotional experience.

    In our own experience, grounding a literary text in personal
subjectivity actually results in a greater attention to the text
itself. Students argue over an author's "idea" or "message."
They refer to the text to establish a viewpoint in opposition to
some other student's. They seek ways to express their "opinion"
about a text and learn that they must substantiate their claim by
showing the class the evidence from the text that supports this
claim.

    We chose as texts for interpretation one by a classic
"master," Anton Chekhov, and the other, by an impressive
contemporary, Toni Cade Bambara. Both stories stimulate, we
believe, the kind of argument about human behavior and language
that enlivens a writing class. Yet we also realize you might have
a story that you think works much better. The activities we apply
to our texts can easily be adapted to discussion and writing on
others.

Purpose

We emphasize the reader's contribution to establishing the meaning of a literary text. The communications triangle highlights this interplay of writer, reader and text and encourages student writers to believe that they can make a contribution to the understanding of others by sharing their point of view either individually or collaboratively. From our own experience, we find peer group discussion and writing activities a highly successful way to get students to engage literary texts and to believe that they have something worth contributing to others.

The difficulties you might encounter in teaching students to use their interpretative skills already in use in so many pragmatic ways are not inconsiderable but also not insurmountable. The compression of language and narrative in the short story poses obvious complexities for students. They need to see how a story purchases its effects on readers, how it works proleptically and retrospectively through nuances of character, imagery and plot.

You might take an introductory approach that tries to consider what they already know about fictions. Take an inventory of the kinds of narratives they are familiar with: fables, parables, anecdotes, jokes, sitcoms, action movies, etc. Ask them to explain a recent film they have seen and elicit from this a brief array of storytelling strategies that work on the screen and that one might also encounter in written texts.

Task: Interpreting a Short Story

Writing on a literary text is, for many students, pretty intimidating work. Most of them are familiar with book reports from high school, but these formulaic summaries--with an "I recommend this book to all teenagers" often tacked on as a grandly evaluative peroration--are virtually worthless for teaching students to approach a story critically. We stress the fact that they are writing for an audience that has already read the story and now wishes to be illuminated about the real significance and impact of the story.

The need to wean students from the tendency to write plot summaries and turn their attention to interpretation can be quickly determined by having them write a brief explanation of a fable or fairy tale you reproduce for students to read in class. Some students will grasp immediately the way the parts of the story cohere and suggest a "meaning" to a reader. Others will see only a chronological ordering of actions or events. You may need to spend more time than you think on just how this narrative can be read and interpreted.

On the other hand, some students see the reading of all literature as a search for a univocal, fixed "message" or "lesson" that assigns a specific function for each element of the story. It can be a genuine eye-opener when students are presented with various possible interpretations of the same text by their own peers and then asked to consider them all as the "right" interpretation. At first this revelation may throw them into immediate confusion but after some practice with reading and writing about stories, even the most literal-minded of students comes around to seeing fiction in a more rewarding way.

Generating Ideas:

All of the activities we suggest--double-entry journals, brainstorming, question sets--are directed to getting students to talk, think, and write about a literary text. Group work can be quite fruitful in accomplishing this. You might duplicate a different short fable, parable or joke for each group, asking the students to explain it or comment on its use of language. Each group can then explain its findings to the whole class and elicit comment from it.

The image of Janus suggests that the process of reading a literary work is not just a simple linear progress from first to last paragraph but a recursive movement marked by the reader's growing awareness of how the different elements in the story work together to create some "pattern of meaning or significance." The meaning of the gooseberries to Ivan's brother is thus expanded into an image of ideal happiness that contains implications broader than the story itself.

As the selections from their journals reveal, students often have some pithy, thoughtful remarks to make on the human values and moral conflicts represented in a work of fiction. It can be quite a different situation with recent modernist or post-modernist authors whose stories attenuate the role of plot, character and theme in their attempts to alert us to other possible narrative devices.

Addressing Your Audience:

We emphasize the personal, social, and cultural perspectives to encourage students to see these stories in as richly detailed a way as the stories can support. You may decide to emphasize one more than the others; each story we read seems to demand a particular emphasis. We spend more time in class discussing the role of social class in "The Lesson" but it is surely an important consideration in "Gooseberries" as well.

You might ask students to freewrite on one of these perspectives or ask them to find analogies with current films or television dramas. Comparing the notion of ideal happiness in the film Pretty Woman with that of "Gooseberries" yielded one class a topic for an animated discussion and writing activity. Although the questions in Some Practice with Reader Perspectives apply only to the two texts we have studied, you can substitute another story--or other kind of work--and ask similar questions about frame of reference and bridging the gaps between interpretations.

Arranging Your Essay:

The shaping idea--whatever relative depth of understanding it reveals--should try to make some worthwhile generalization about the story. As we suggest, this generalization might come at the end of the writer's examination of his or her own reading process, "the reader's story" of a reader reading. This process can lead students to evaluate their own generalizations and use of evidence from the text. The writer of "A Blind Man's Dream" arrives at a conclusion about the destructive power of greed, an insight that might be further developed in another draft of an essay.

The "writer's repertoire" encourages students to consider a number of ways to develop an interpretive essay. You might take one student's tentative shaping idea and try to; effective pattern of development from the class, in effect asking the question "How can I best explain or convey this insight?"

The writer of "No Man Is an Island" doesn't discuss any of the formal elements of Chekhov's storytelling but does offer an impassioned criticism of life. You might discuss this draft with your class, asking them how effectively it has revealed the thematic concerns of the story to them, and what else the writer could have explained about the way the story works as a story.

Focus on Form and Style:

This brief discussion of some of the elements of the short story, as they apply to our reading of Chekhov and Bambara, are not intended as a primer for reading interpretatively. They try to reflect some of the concerns a reader might encounter, and they offer some suggestions about what might be considered in writing an essay on a work of short fiction.

Clearly, Chekhov's and Bambara`s stories are worlds apart in terms of social milieu, language and scope. But part of the interest in writing on stories is seeing just how a "yoking of opposites" can form a revelation of meaning for readers who see, for example, how much potential loss of spontaneity and feeling may be in store for Sylvia if, like Ivan's brother, she sacrifices her openness of feeling for the pursuit of social acceptance and material well-being and becomes another Miss Moore in the process.

You might focus on one of the narrative elements discussed in this section, inquiring with your class to see just how significant it is for the telling of the tale. This can become the topic of an essay that examines the role of, say, irony in "Gooseberries" or point of view in "The Lesson."

The questions in "Some Practice with Interpreting 'Gooseberries' and 'The Lesson'" ask students to consider how the opening of a story can yield valuable insight into the makeup of the whole (Exercise 1); Chekhov's choice of narrator (Exercise 2); Bambara's choice of narrator (Exercise 3); how narratives are created and how they are formed into a plot (Exercise 4); how to recognize crucial scenes in terms of their cinematic qualities (Exercise 5); how to imagine alternative ways of rendering familiar narratives (Exercise 6); how students' outside reading can be enhanced by their understanding of narrative elements (Exercise 7).

Rewriting:

The revised draft of "No Man Is an Island" has taken into account some but not all of the peer responses. The writer has balanced the contrast of the two brothers by considering Ivan's limitations but hasn't really stepped back from the foreground of character and plot in order to build a larger generalization about Chekhov's treatment of the gap that separates human aspirations from accomplishments. You might practice writing out brief generalizations of the theme of this story with your class, stressing that these could become the shaping ideas of their final drafts.

You might compare the checklist of questions for revising with the drafts that students have written, assigning specific questions to peer groups for consideration. Going over the checklist can reveal gaps in students' attention to the major concerns of the story that can be filled in at this point in the writing process.

Becoming Aware of Yourself as a Writer:

Several of these questions ask students to reflect on the process of writing about literature that they have just completed. We also ask them to consider what connections with their lives they perceive the fiction might have. A third set of questions directs them to the bearing this task might have on their writing about other literature as well as the extent to which their previous encounters with poetry, drama, and fiction might contribute to their fulfilling of the chapter task.

Sample Syllabi

Below are two sample syllabi, one for a 15-week
semester, the other for a 10-week semester. Neither covers
every chapter of Ways to Writing completely. Experience has
taught us that it is expecting too much of both students and
instructors to assign in a single semester a journal plus ten
essays, each essay developed into final form through a minimum of
one rough draft, and in many cases, through two or three such
drafts. Particularly if students are expected to work through the
lessons in rhetoric and through selected exercises as
thoroughly as possible, it is probably reasonable to ask them
to produce no more than one finished essay every two weeks.
The research and persuasive tasks may require an additional
week. Hence, in the sample syllabi below, although material
from every chapter is assigned, only five final essays are
actually required in the 10-week semester, six in the 15-week
semester.

Note that in these syllabi, each week's work includes
three sections of classroom activities, three sections of
assignments. The assumption is that, in general, composition
courses meet three hours per week, whether once for three
hours, twice for an hour and one-half, or three times for an
hour. There is in each syllabus enough time scheduled to
offer you the opportunity to intervene in the various stages
of the writing process, particularly to review your students'
rough drafts.

The bulk of the class time in these syllabi is divided
between what we term "discussion" and peer group work.
Discussion may involve some lecture as well as the sort of
question and answer sessions that tend to characterize class
discussions. But certainly much of the work scheduled for
these discussions lends itself to peer group sessions if you
prefer to stress a workshop approach more than our sample
syllabi do.

Note also that different exercises are often assigned
for the same chapters covered in the 15-week and the 10-week
syllabi. Some exercises obviously will take a student more
time, for example those that ask the student to write one or
more paragraphs. Such exercises tend to be assigned more
often in the 15-week syllabus, simply because of the time
factor. Further, some exercises are best discussed in peer
groups, for example those having to do with evaluating
audience point of view in Chapter 3. When such exercises are
assigned in the syllabi below, they are scheduled for peer
group work. You will find, however, that many of the other
exercises scheduled for class discussion also lend themselves

to group work.

15-Week Syllabus (Includes Introduction: Ways to Writing, Tasks
in Chapters 1-2 combined, 5, 7, 8-9 combined, 10, 11)

Week 1

Class 1 - Introduction to the Course
    Assignment - Read Introduction: Ways to Writing.
Class 2 - Discussion of the writing process and of keeping a
    journal.
    Assignment - Read Introduction to Part I on expressive
    writing and the sections in Chapter 1 on Purpose and
    Generating Ideas: Free Writing. Exercises in Some Practice
    in Starting Your Journal. Begin keeping a daily journal.
Class 3 - Discussion of expressive writing and the sample journal
    entries in the Generating Ideas section. Discussion of
    students' experiences with free writing and with journal
    writing.
    Assignment - Read the Audience section in Chapter 1 and do
    exercises in Some Practice With Voice.

Week 2

Class 1 - Discussion of private voice and the exercises in the
    Audience section.
    Assignment - Read Establishing Your Point of View and do
    exercises in Some Practice With Your Point of View. In
    journal, answer Becoming Aware of Yourself as a Writer
    questions.
Class 2 - Discussion of Point of View exercises. Group
    discussions of issues implicit in Becoming Aware of Yourself
    as a Writer.
    Assignment - Read the Purpose and Generating Ideas sections
    in Chapter 2. Do exercises for Some Practice in Tracing a
    Pattern in Your Journal. Read Addressing Your Audience: The
    Sympathetic Reader and do five exercises at end in your
    journal.
Class 3 - Discussion of Tracing a Pattern in Your Journal and
    Addressing a Sympathetic Reader.
    Assignment - Read Arranging the Essay, Writing Your Rough
    Draft, and Focus on Form: Stating a Thesis/Writing an
    Introduction.

Week 3

Class 1 - Discussion of Stating a Thesis, Arranging the Essay, and
    Writing Your Rough Draft.
    Assignment - Write a rough draft of an essay based on a
    pattern in your journal.

Class 2 - Group work to critique rough drafts.
   Assignment - Read Rewriting section and revise rough draft.
   Answer Becoming Aware of Yourself as a Writer questions in
   your journal.
Class 3 - Publication, reading, and discussion of selected final
   drafts. Group work on Becoming Aware questions.
   Assignment - Read Introduction to Part II on exploratory
   writing. In Chapter 5, read Purpose, Task, and Generating
   Ideas sections. Do exercises at end of Generating Ideas.

Week 4

Class 1 - Discussion of exploratory writing and the task of
   exploring and writing about a prejudgment. Discussion of the
   classical questions and exercises.
   Assignment - Read Addressing Your Audience: Writing for
   Publication and do exercises at end.
Class 2 - Discussion of writing for publication.
   Assignment - Read Arranging Your Essay and Writing Your Rough
   Draft sections.
Class 3 - Discussion of arrangement patterns as well as of
   professional and student models.
   Assignment - Read Focus on Form sections in Chapters 3, 4 and
   5 on paragraphs, conclusions, and sentence combining.

Week 5

Class 1 - Discussion of paragraphing, writing conclusions, and
   combining sentences.
   Assignment - Write a rough draft of your essay on a
   prejudgment.
Class 2 - Group work to critique rough drafts.
   Assignment - Read Rewriting section and revise rough draft.
   Answer questions in Becoming Aware of Yourself as a Writer in
   your journal.
Class 3 - Publication, reading, and discussion of selected final
   drafts. Group work on Becoming Aware questions.
   Assignment - Read Introduction to Part III on explanatory
   writing. In Chapter 7, read Purpose, Task, and Generating
   Ideas sections. Do exercises at end of Generating Ideas.

Week 6

Class 1 - Discussion of explanatory writing and the task of
   explaining and writing about the media. Discussion of
   generating ideas through generalization.
   Assignment - Read Addressing Your Audience: Adopting a
   Public Voice. Do exercises at end.
Class 2 - Discussion of the elements of a public voice, including
   Edwin Newman's essay.

Assignment - Read Arranging Your Essay and Writing Your Rough Draft sections.

Class 3 - Discussion of arrangement patterns as well as of professional and student models.
Assignment - Write a rough draft of your essay on a prejudgment.

Week 7

Class 1 - Group work to critique rough drafts.
Assignment - Read Focus on Style sections in Chapters 6 and 7.

Class 2 - Discussion of eliminating deadwood and of the components of style.
Assignment - Read Rewriting section and revise rough draft, paying particular attention to style. Answer Becoming Aware of Yourself as a Writer questions in your journal.

Class 3 - Publication, reading, and discussion of selected final drafts. Group work on Becoming Aware questions.
Assignment - Read Introduction to Part IV on persuasive writing. In Chapter 8, read Purpose and Task sections.

Week 8

Class 1 - Discussion of persuasive writing and the task of creating a case and arguing your point of view. (Note: instead of having students create their own cases, you may want them to choose one of the national debates in Chapter 9 and argue from one of the points of view on the issue.)
Assignment - Read the Generating Ideas section. Do exercises throughout the Generating Ideas section.

Class 2 and 3 - Discussion of the logical appeal by generating ideas through strategies for argument, induction, deduction and the classical questions.
Assignment - Read Persuading Your Audience. Do exercises throughout.

Week 9

Class 1 - Discussion of the ethical appeal: establishing credibility and adopting the proper tone.
Assignment - Read Arranging Your Essay and Writing Your Rough Draft sections.

Class 2 - Discussion of arrangement patterns as well as of professional and student models.
Assignment - Write a rough draft of your essay on a prejudgment.

Class 3 - Group work to critique rough drafts.
Assignment - Read Focus on Style section on the Appeal to the Emotions. Do exercises.

Class 1 - Discussion of connotation, denotation, figurative
language, allusion, repetition, and other elements of the
persuasive style.
<u>Assignment</u> - Read Rewriting section and revise rough draft.
Answer questions on Becoming Aware of Yourself as a Writer in
your journal.
Class 2 - Publication, reading, and discussion of selected final
drafts. Group work on Becoming Aware questions.
<u>Assignment</u> - Read Introduction to Part V on writing about
reading. In Chapter 10, read Purpose and Task sections.
Class 3 - (Note: As the task for this chapter calls for a
research paper, you may want either to schedule the first
four assignments--through gathering sources and taking notes-
-earlier in the term or to make the paper due nearer the end
of the semester. Discussion of research and the task of
testing a hypothesis.
<u>Assignment</u> - Read the Generating Ideas section. Do both sets
of exercises at the end.

Week <u>11</u>

Class 1 - Discussion of the role of induction in scientific
thinking. Discussion of evidence.
<u>Assignment</u> - Read Addressing Your Audience: The Lay Reader,
plus exercises.
Class 2 - Discussion of writing for the lay reader. <u>Assignment</u> -
Read section on Doing Research, including Finding a Topic,
Gathering Sources, and Taking Notes. Do exercises on
research methods.
Class 3 - Discussion of finding a topic, gathering sources, and
using summary, paraphrase, and quotation in taking notes.
<u>Assignment</u> - Read Arranging Your Essay.

Week <u>12</u>

Class 1 - Discussion of stating the hypothesis, outlining, putting
notes together, writing the introduction, and writing the
rough draft. Discuss student model.
<u>Assignment</u> - Read Focus on Form: Documentation. Do
exercises.
Class 2 - Discuss documentation.
<u>Assignment</u> - Write a rough draft of your research essay.
Class 3 - Group work to critique rough drafts.
<u>Assignment</u> - Read Rewriting section and revise your rough
draft. Answer questions on Becoming Aware of Yourself as a
Writer in your journal.

<u>Week</u> <u>13</u>

Class 1 - Publication, reading, and discussion of selected student
     research papers. Group work on Becoming Aware questions.
     <u>Assignment</u> - In Chapter 11, read Purpose and Task sections,
     including two short stories.
Class 2 - Discussion of two stories.
     <u>Assignment</u> - Read Generating Ideas section on Reader
     Responses. Do exercises at end of Generating Ideas.
Class 3 - Discuss the active reader.
     <u>Assignment</u> - Read Addressing Your Audience: Reader
     Perspectives. Do exercises at end.

<u>Week</u> <u>14</u>

Class 1 - Discussion of reader points of view and reader frames of
     reference.
     <u>Assignment</u> - Read Arranging Your Essay and Writing Your Rough
     Draft sections.
Class 2 - Discussion of arrangement patterns as well as of student
     models.
     <u>Assignment</u> - Read Focus on Form and Style: The Elements of a
     Short Story.
Class 3 - Discussion of plot, character, point of view, theme, and
     irony.
     <u>Assignment</u> - Prepare a rough draft of your essay interpreting
     a short story.

<u>Week</u> <u>15</u>

Class 1 - Group work to critique rough drafts.
     <u>Assignment</u> - Read Rewriting section and revise your rough
     draft. Answer Becoming Aware of Yourself as a Writer
     questions in your journal.
Class 2 - Publication, reading, and discussion of final drafts.
     Group work on Becoming Aware questions.
Class 3 - Final exam, if required.

<u>10-Week</u> <u>Syllabus</u> (Includes Tasks for Chapters 1-2 combined, 3, 4,
5, and 8)

<u>Week</u> <u>1</u>

Class 1 Introduction to the course and diagnostic essay.
     <u>Assignment</u> - Read the Introduction: Ways To Writing and
     the subsection on Generating Ideas: Free Writing in the
     section on Writing Your Journal in Chapter 1. Write
     out exercises 3 and 4 in More Practice with Free
     Writing.

Class 2 Group work on and discussion of individual writing
        processes and free writing.
        Assignment - Read Introduction to Part I. Also read in
        Chapter 1 sections on Purpose and Task as well as
        subsections on Starting a Journal and Keeping a Journal
        in the section on Writing Your Journal. Begin keeping a
        journal with exercises 1 and 3 in Some Practice in
        Starting Your Journal.
Class 3 Discussion of the sample journal entries in
        Chapter 1. Group work on possible subjects for journal
        writing.
        Assignment - Read subsection on Addressing Your
        Audience: Private Voice in Chapter 1 and write out
        exercises 3 and 6 in Some Practice with Voice along with
        exercise 1 in Some Practice with Your Point of View.
        Also read the subsection on Addressing Your Audience:
        The "Intended" Reader(s) in the section on Writing Your
        Essay in Chapter 3.

Week 2

Class 1 Discussion of point of view and writing for an
        audience. Group work on exercises in Some Practice with
        a Reader's Frame of Reference and Some Practice with a
        Reader's Point of View in the audience subsection in
        Chapter 3.
        Assignment - Read the Purpose sections in Chapters 2 and
        3. In Chapter 3 read Task: Writing About an Incident
        and the subsection on Generating Ideas: The
        Journalist's Questions in the section on Writing Your
        Essay. Do exercise 4 in Some Practice with the
        Journalist's Questions.
 Class 2 Discussion of journalist's questions. Group work
        on generating ideas about an incident to write on.
        Assignment - Read subsections on Arranging Your Essay:
        The Shaping Idea, Narration, and Exposition, and Writing
        Your Rough Draft in the section on Writing Your Essay in
        Chapter 3. Brainstorm in your journal a list of ideas
        for an essay on an incident.
Class 3 Group Work on followed by class discussion of "The
        Angry Winter."
        Assignment - Write a rough draft of your essay on an
        incident. Read subsection on Writing Your Rough Draft
        in Chapter 2 along with the section on Focus on Form:
        Stating a Thesis/Writing and Introduction.

Week 3

Class 1 Group work on shaping idea for your essay on an
        incident. Discussion of sample introductions in Focus

section of Chapter 2.

Assignment - Read Focus on Form: Paragraph
Structure/Making Transitions in Chapter 3. Write out
exercises 1 - 3 in Some Practice with Paragraph
Structure and exercise 2 in Some Practice with Paragraph
Structure in Your Essay on an Incident. Also do
exercise 1 in Some Practice with Transitions.

Class 2 Group work on assigned exercises. Discussion of
paragraph structure and transitions in "Moma's Private
Victory" and "One night I was awakened by a phone
call...."

Assignment - Read subsections on Working in a Peer Group
on Revising, Revising, and The Final Product in the
section on Rewriting in Chapter 2 and the Rewriting
section in Chapter 3. Prepare a rough draft of your
essay on an incident for peer critique.

Class 3 Peer group work on revising your essay on an
incident.

Assignment - Revise your essay on an incident and
prepare it for submission. Respond in your journal to
the following questions in Becoming Aware of Yourself as
a Writer: in Chapter 1, questions 1, 2, and 5; in
Chapter 2, question 2 and 3; in Chapter 3, questions 1,
2, and 6. Read the Introduction to Part II.

Week 4

Class 1 Submit your essay on an incident. Two volunteers
will present their final drafts for class discussion.
Discussion of responses to Becoming Aware of Yourself as
a Writer and of the difference between Expression and
Exploration as a writer's aim.

Assignment - Read sections on Purpose and Task in
Chapter 4. Also read subsections on Generating Ideas:
The Explorer's Questions and Addressing Your Audience:
Depth of Information in the section on Writing Your
Essay in Chapter 4. Write out exercise 1 in some
Practice with Using the Explorer's Questions to Generate
Ideas About a Place.

Class 2 Discussion of the explorer's questions and of
possible subjects for writing about a place.

Assignment - Read Arranging Your Essay and Writing Your
Rough Draft in the section on Writing Your Essay in
Chapter 4.

Class 3 Group work on questions following "On a Kibbutz."
Discussion of arrangement patterns in "On a Kibbutz" and
"The Iowa State Fair."

Assignment - Visit the place that you intend to write
about for Chapter 4's task. Write out exercises 1 - 3
in Using Your Journal in Answering the Explorer's

Questions About a Place and exercise 2 in Some Practice
in Determining Your Audience's Depth of Information for
Your Essay on a Place. Read Focus on Form: Paragraph
Development/Writing Your Conclusion.

Week 5

Class 1 In-class exercises on Some Practice with Developing
Paragraphs. Discussion of arrangement and paragraph
development in student essay "Paying for a Higher
Education."
Assignment - Write out exercise 2 in Some Practice with
Writing a Conclusion for Your Essay About a Place.
Prepare a draft of your essay on a place for peer group
critique.
Class 2 Peer group work on revising your essay on a place.
Assignment - Read Rewriting section in chapter 4.
Revise your essay on a place and prepare it for
submission. Answer the questions in Becoming Aware of
Yourself as a Writer at the end of Chapter 4.
Class 3 Submit your essay on a place. Two volunteers will
submit their final drafts for class discussion.
Discussion of responses to Becoming Aware of Yourself as
a Writer.
Assignment - Read Introduction to Part III, sections on
Purpose and Task in Chapter 6, and the subsections on
Generating Ideas: The Classical Questions and
Generating Ideas: Brainstorming in Chapters 5 and 6.
Write out exercises 1 and 2 in Some Practice with
Listing, exercise 1 in Some Practice with Clustering,
and exercise 1 in Some Practice with Using the
Explorer's and Classical Questions in Brainstorming.

Week 6

Class 1 Discussion of Exploratory vs. Explanatory Aims and of
the Task for Chapter 6. Group work on assigned
exercises on brainstorming and clustering.
Assignment - Write out exercises 1 - 5 in Some Practice
with Brainstorming to Generate Ideas for Your Essay on a
Tradition. Read the subsection on Addressing Your
Audience: Considering the Values and Attitudes of the
Uninformed Reader in Chapter 6. Write out exercise 1 in
Some Practice with Writing on a Tradition for an
Uninformed Reader.
Class 2 Discussion of writing for an uniformed reader.
Group work on generating a subject for your essay on a
tradition.
Assignment - Read subsections on Arranging Your Essay
and Writing Your Rough Draft in the section on Writing

Your Essay in Chapter 6. Write out exercise 2 in Some
Practice in Writing on a Tradition for an Uninformed
Reader.

Class 3 Group work on and discussion of questions 1 - 6
following "On Being Black and Middle Class."
Assignment - Write a rough draft for peer critique of
your essay on a tradition. Read Focus on Style:
Eliminating Deadwood in Chapter 6.

Week 7

Class 1 Peer group work on revising your essay on a
tradition.
Assignment - Write out exercise 2 in Some Practice with
Eliminating Deadwood in Your Essay on a Tradition. Read
the Rewriting section in Chapter 6. Also read the
subsection on Distributing in the Rewriting section of
Chapter 5. Work on revising your essay on a tradition.

Class 2 Discussion of revision of student essay "House of
Delight." One or two volunteers will present their
revision-in-progress to the class for discussion.
Assignment - Prepare final draft of your essay on a
tradition for submission. Write in your journal your
responses to the questions in Becoming Aware of Yourself
as a Writer at the end of Chapter 6.

Class 3 Submit your essay on a tradition. Discussion of
responses to Becoming Aware of Yourself as a Writer.
Assignment - Read the Introduction to Part IV. In
Chapter 8, read the sections on Purpose and Task and the
subsection on Generating Ideas: Strategies for
Argument, Induction, Deduction, and the Classical
Questions in the section on Writing Your Essay. Write
out exercises 1, 2, and 5 in Some Practice with
Induction.

Week 8

Class 1 Discussion of persuasive aims and strategies of
argument. Group work on brainstorming ideas for an
issue about which you might argue your point of view.
Assignment - Write out exercises 1 - 4 in Some Practice
with Generating Ideas to Argue Your Point of View. Read
the subsection on Persuading Your Audience in Chapter 8.
Write out exercises 1 and 2 in some Practice with Using
the Ethical Appeal in Arguing Your Point of View.

Class 2 Group work in which members role-play the audience
for one another's case.
Assignment - Read the subsections on Addressing Your
Audience: Adopting a Public Voice and Addressing Your
Audience: The Informed Reader in the sections on

Writing Your Essay in Chapters 7 and 9. Write out exercise 1 in Some Practice with a Public Voice and exercise 3 in Some Practice with Writing for an Informed Audience.

Class 3 Group work on assigned exercises. Discussion of the attitude toward audience exhibited by Edwin Newman in "What Effect Is TV Having on the Evolution of English?" and by Lewis Thomas in "The Lives of a Cell."
Assignment - Read the subsections on Arranging Your Essay and Writing Your Rough Draft in the section on Writing Your Essay in Chapter 8. Write a rough draft of your essay on an issue.

Week 9

Class 1 Peer group work on revising your essay on an issue.
Assignment - Read Focus on Style: Persuasive Language and the Appeal to the Emotions and the section on Rewriting in Chapter 8. Write out exercises 1, 2, and 6 in Some Practice with Appealing to the Emotions of the Reader of Your Persuasive Essay.

Class 2 Discussion of persuasive language in "Letter from a Birmingham Jail" and in "Bodybuilding: The Shape of the Future."
Assignment - Revise your essay on an issue and prepare it for submission. Write in your journal your responses to the questions in Becoming Aware of Yourself as a Writer at the end of Chapter 8.

Class 3 Submit your essay on an issue. Discussion of responses to Becoming Aware of Yourself as a Writer.
Assignment - Read the sections on Task and Writing Your Essay in Chapter 2. Begin reading over your journal.

Week 10

Class 1 Group work on brainstorming about a pattern of thought or feeling in the journal entries of Thoreau and Angela S. in Chapter 2. Discussion of the main point of their respective essays.
Assignment - Write a draft of an essay on a pattern of thoughts about writing that emerges from your journal.

Class 2 Peer group work on revision of your final essay.
Assignment - Prepare your final essay for submission.

Class 3 Submit your journal and your final essay on the pattern of thoughts about writing that emerges from your journal.

WAYS TO TEACHING--SUGGESTED STRATEGIES

Assigning a Journal

Most writing instructors recognize that there is an inherent value in having their students keep a journal. But questions arise about the relationship between journal writing and the more formal writing assignments of the course. The answers to such questions lie, in part, in clearly defining the uses that the journal can be put to in the writing classroom.

The journal, of course, may be assigned simply to get students to write more than they ordinarily would, even during a semester in which they are taking a writing course. But it also may be used in ways specifically related to the formal essays and other exercises assigned in such a course.

Why Assign the Journal. We think it is a good idea to have students keep a daily journal throughout the semester, simply to accustom them to setting down their feelings and thoughts on paper. Whether, for a set amount of time each day, they are writing freely about whatever comes to mind or with a focus suggested by you as the instructor, the act of keeping a journal can kelp make the writing process more habitual and so less alien to many students.

Some instructors question the value of asking students to write freely in their journal, especially if that writing remains private, a matter solely between the student and him- or herself. We feel, however, that many students, inhibited by the pressures of criticism and grading, can benefit from the opportunity the journal affords them to discover and ponder themselves, their thoughts, and the style in which they express their thoughts and emotions. If the journal is assigned for such reasons, you may not ask to look at what the students are writing in it at all; or, you may require students to submit selections periodically throughout the semester or at semester's end, thus encouraging them to write as freely and openly as possible while still monitoring their work.

The journal may also be assigned with more expository purposes in mind. You may ask students to write an analysis of a reading assignment, for example, or a summary of a lesson, or an evaluation of comments received on a paper. Again, while there is value in keeping such journal work private, students do learn how to develop and clarify ideas about a reading assignment or about how to revise a paper by sharing such work with other classmates; and you may ask to look at such journal work simply to check that students are doing it or to initiate further discussion of the

101

writing process, for example of how ideas that first appear in a journal entry are utilized in successive drafts of an essay.

How to Use the Journal in a Writing Class. The journal then can have a variety of uses in a writing class. The instructor who would stress the importance of expressive writing may ask students to use the journal, at least at first, as a sort of private diary. The instructor who would direct students' attention to more expository modes may ask students to keep a journal as a kind of notebook of ideas gathered from observation, discussion, and reading. The instructor who would have students focus on abstract rhetorical principles may ask them to use the journal as a place to summarize and raise questions about lessons taught in class, to write out exercises that reinforce such lessons, and to generate ideas for essay assignments. In all three cases, the journal becomes a form through which the student writer is constantly asked to study the relationship between writing and thinking. It is this relationship that the journal work in Ways to Writing is intended to stress.

In Ways to Writing, the journal is introduced first as a means for the student writer to express her-or himself in private. The task for Chapter 1 requires that students keep a journal in which they write about themselves for at least two to three weeks (see the notes on Chapter 1 in the preceding section on Chapter Notes). We thus suggest that you assign the journal in some form during the first week of class and encourage students to keep and utilize their journal daily throughout the semester. By completing the task for Chapter 1, students learn how the journal can be both a place to explore their skills (and their weaknesses) as writers and a primary source of ideas for an essay. We suggest the journal be used as well as a means of generating ideas for later tasks, for selected exercises throughout the book, and for the questions in the last section of each chapter of Becoming Aware of Yourself as a Writer. Thus, from the start, the journal provides a written format in which students are encouraged to constantly reevaluate their own writing.

In subsequent chapters, the journal can continue to be utilized in theses ways. While in each chapter after the second, different heuristic devices are introduced, the prewriting activities of the Generating Ideas and Audience sections can continue to be done in the journal. In several chapters (3, 4, 5), for example, the journal can become a kind of reporter's notebook, while in the later chapters, it can serve as a repository of information and ideas about various subjects. Thus, sharing of the journal at the stage of generating ideas may be introduced in group work early in the semester, starting even with the second chapter, if you encourage a focus on material that is not deeply personal or if the students are willing to share such material with one another before it is revised and edited for a formal essay. Class or peer group discussion of how a writer might make alterations in journal material before including it in a formal essay is one way of reinforcing the lessons of the Audience section of each chapter.

If the journal is used in these ways, we have found that it can help students develop material for essays, make adjustments in their writing for specific audiences, and pay closer attention to problems of style and structure. The journal becomes a primary tool for introducing students to all stages of the writing process through the act of writing, assisting them at the same time in developing a firmer sense of control over the final product that emerges from this process.

Using Professional and Student Model Essays

Both professional and student essays are included as a way of answering students' question "What will an essay for this task look like?" The models also offer possible solutions to specific recurrent problems students have with writing such as what to write about, how to formulate a thesis, how to develop a topic, how to arrange the material, how to write for a reader, how to revise, and so forth.

Students can also be asked to recreate the writer's own process in grappling with the rhetorical situation, particularly each student's process in completion of the chapter's task.

Structuring the Classroom: Roles of Teacher and Student

Workshop Approach. Way to Writing does not insist on any particular classroom structure or on any particular roles for teacher and student. However, our experience in teaching the book in its various stages of progress over the past eleven years has suggested that the classroom become primarily a workshop in which students work together, by themselves, and both individually and collectively with the instructor to learn the craft of writing.

We have found that the Purpose, Task, Generating Ideas, Audience, and Writing the Essay sections do lend themselves to some lecture but only in conjunction with discussion and group or individual workshop endeavors as well. The Revising section requires a workshop approach if students are to critique each others' drafts as does the class period in which students share their "published" final drafts with their classmates.

The Role of Teacher and Student. The role of student is that of any workshop member come to learn a craft. Students must be learners, creators, collaborators, critics, instigators, questioners, listeners, teachers: the roles are numerous and varied.

The role of teacher that we suggest is that of workshop leader, a role new for some who are used to the traditional role of teacher as imparter of knowledge, critic, talker, questioner, answerer. In the classroom suggested by Ways to Writing and the new rhetoric in general, the instructor becomes much more: in fact, the instructor takes on many of the roles ascribed above to students: learner, creator, collaborator, listener. Both instructor and student share, in other words, in the many roles necessary for this workshop approach. And while the teacher remains final arbiter of the writing that is done, he or she should be so only in the sense of being a more experienced writer, an editor-in-chief, so to speak.

Setting Up Peer Groups. We have worked with peer groups as the main component of our workshop approach for over a decade. We have tried elaborate methods of organizing these groups, and we have also grouped students very informally, and have found that groups tend to function efficiently regardless of how they are formed.

For the instructor first attempting to organize a class into groups, a more elaborate approach may seem more satisfying. Most teachers who have not experimented with groups feel that turning over classtime to students will result in chaos, and may welcome any attempt to create order out of potential disorder. (We discuss below the corresponding issue of whether students learn by working in groups.)

Carefully structuring peer groups requires heterogeneous groupings. Groups should consist of males and females, good writers and weaker writers, extroverted and introverted personalities, and various ages and ethnic backgrounds if these vary in your class. Since we have found it helpful to form our groups as early in the semester as possible so that students can quickly adapt to the idea that other students will critique their writing and work with them on other phases of the production of each essay, we therefore obtain writing samples as early in the semester as possible in order to sort the various writing abilities. Just a few class discussions are needed to distinguish between the types of personalities in the class and among the ages and/or amounts of experience of the students.

After a few class meetings, you will probably also have some idea of who might be a good group leader: a student who is responsible; firm, if not extroverted; and a good writer. A group leader acts as your surrogate with his or her peers and also a liaison between you and the other group members.

Depending on the group activities you organize, you may also want each group to have a secretary or recorder who will record the group's discussion for distribution to the members of the group or to you. The recorder position is useful too in assuring the democracy of the group and in sharing the responsibilities of the group leadership.

Groups should not be larger than four, at the most five students. Since one purpose of group work is to encourage all students to become active in the class, groups must be kept small both to allow and to encourage all members to participate. Also, the mechanics of peer critiquing are more easily managed with a smaller number: fewer copies need be made, fewer class periods need be allotted to in-class critiquing (a maximum of two essays can be critiqued in one fifty-minute class period), and for out-of-class critiquing, students have fewer essays to evaluate.

When early writing samples indicate that most students in a class are fairly good writers, a more informal method of group organization may be tried. Often simply assigning students in a class of 24 numbers from 1-6 will produce groups of four that function as well as those with more design. Grouping students alphabetically will work also. A leader will usually emerge from this informal arrangement, although in a homogeneous class, groups often function democratically with everyone sharing responsibility for the work.

Should the dynamics of a group simply not encourage productive encounters (you will know a group is dysfunctional either through members' complaints or through their oral or written reports), you may want to shift students among groups. We warn you, however, that unless students simply cannot work with each other, they will resist any group reformulation; bonding takes place very quickly, and any shifts must be made very early in the semester.

Once students have accepted that you expect them to learn from each other, that in fact they <u>can</u> learn from each other, you do not need to supervise them. In fact, they will function <u>best</u> if you do not monitor or participate in their groups; the responsibility for completing the group task grants them power and authority.

<u>Group Activities</u>. Students can be asked to work in groups whenever a workshop approach seems required: in helping each other generate ideas, formulate a topic from the task, analyze the audience, and arrange and write the essay. We have made specific suggestions as to group activities in the notes on each chapter.

Groups, of course, have as their main purpose the critiquing of each other's writing at its various stages. The mechanics of critiquing can vary. Students can simply read their drafts aloud to each other, or they can bring in xeroxed copies for others to read. Writing can be critiqued in class or outside of class.

We have found it useful to have the Audience Response Guide duplicated so that students can write their responses on the sheet and hand it to the writer; this can be done, as we have indicated, either in or out of class.

In conducting in-class critiquing sessions, we have always followed Peter Elbow's advice in <u>Writing Without Teachers</u>: if reading aloud, read twice, allowing time after each reading for group members to collect and note their thoughts. Allow time for two silent readings as well. In sharing their evaluations with the writer, readers cannot be argued with, either by the writer or by other readers; everyone--both reader and writer--is always right and always wrong. Writers will not, in fact, respond to comments at all but simply contemplate the value for their writing of the critiques given.

An alternative approach is to encourage the writer to formulate questions about areas of difficulty in writing the essay to which the group can respond.

Teaching Revision

The profession has come a long way from the days, chronologically not so long ago, when allowing students to revise their essays seemed somehow like encouraging them to cheat, as if we were giving them a chance to resuscitate after the execution. Now, research--if not common sense--has shown us that since experienced writers including ourselves fill wastebaskets with draft after draft or constantly revise and edit on the computer, the inexperienced writers in our classrooms should be encouraged to do so also--and with guidance along the way.

Our blessing is not sufficient, however. How do we teach them to revise--who to receive feedback from, what to revise, when to revise, how to revise, even why to revise? Research and experience are providing some valuable teaching tools.

<u>Why Revise</u>. One way to teach students the need for revision is to show them various drafts you have written in the pursuit of a particular writing goal. Duplicate for them your successive starts and show them how you progressed to a draft with which you were finally pleased. Let them see an experienced writer at work, seeking to clarify thinking and improve communication with the reader.

Another approach to demonstrating the necessity for revision is to have each group or the class as a whole write an essay on a topic of interest to all. Drawing from the students their sense of how to better organize and articulate what has been contributed will convey to everyone the potentially vast number of choices available as well as those that are preferable to the task at hand.

For those students who tend to freeze when faced with a blank page, the realization that a first effort does not have to be perfect may help to prevent writer's block.

In Chapter 2 we have presented three successive stages of student writing from journal pages to a rough draft based on the ideas generated there to the draft that the student handed in for final evaluation. By tracing these successive stages, students should be able to see the improvements in presentation that were made. Likewise, the two drafts in the other chapters will give students other perceptions of what can be accomplished through revision.

Who Provides Feedback. In Ways to Writing we have suggested that students can learn best what to revise by seeking out readers for feedback--either themselves (the writer as reader), their peers, or their instructors, or perhaps ideally all three.

Whether the student is writing for a particular audience or for herself or himself alone, feedback is essential for inexperienced writers because they are so often unable, as Macrorie says, to tell what they mean even to themselves. We have emphasized peer feedback believing that students learn most easily from the responses of their peers; they have a tendency to ignore the comments of teachers for one reason or another, and they have not yet acquired the reading skills necessary to revise their own work successfully.

Many instructors do not believe that students can successfully intervene in each other's writing processes and suggest useful changes in each other's work. Our experience, however, has been that students certainly are able to do so, and research has been bearing us out.

Those of our colleagues who are skeptical about peer critiquing possibilities are so because since only a few students in a class have "error free" prose, they consider that the deaf will be leading the blind. Assuming that the meaning of a piece of writing takes precedence over stylistic and other surface features at a rough draft stage, then we can also assume that students are well able to comment on the problems of meaning inherent in their peers' work. If surface features are considered as one of the last concerns of the writing process, then students can be asked to intervene at earlier stages when meaning is the focus of the writer's attention. The instructor thus remains the chief commentator on style, grammar, and mechanics.

There are, of course, limits to peer feedback, if only because it is not always available in writing situations. Donald Murray strongly advocates students' development of their "other self" (College English, May 1982). Since writing and reading are inseparable activities, at least for the writer, the "other self" must learn to keep track of what is taking place as the writer writes, achieve a distance from what is being written, provide an evolving context, articulate the problems that have arisen and their solution if any, determine if what is going on "works", and generally provide feedback. It has been our experience that once students have engaged in peer evaluation groups, where other actual selves are responding to their work, they are able to internalize the response of the peer reader and to go a long way in developing their own sense of the direction their writing needs to follow.

What we would suggest is the use of peer group evaluation for perhaps half of the tasks (Chapters One through Four) and then the alternation between peer and self-feedback for the remaining tasks (Chapters Five through Eleven). In this ways, students will begin with external prods, then learn to internalize them with occasional reinforcement from their peers.

As instructor, you might also want to comment on the various stages your student writers are passing through whether that stage is formulating a specific topic, generating ideas, analyzing and writing for the intended audience, or writing the essay. Your intervention need not require inordinate amounts of your time: commenting during the prewriting stages can occur in class discussions or during workshop periods. In commenting on early drafts, you may use the Audience Response Guide or devise your own approach to commenting. You may write your comments on the Guide form, in the margins of their essays, or offer them to the student in conference. If the evaluation takes place during a conference, then the evaluation need not take more time than is required to read the draft and give it some consideration. Most importantly, you will be assisting students in clarifying and perhaps expanding their meaning, thus insuring a superior final product for you to formally evaluate.

When to Revise. Much is being made in the profession of whether the writing process is linear or recursive. To some extent, the distinction is academic since all students are constantly changing their minds at the prewriting stages, hopefully honing their subject and their approach as they proceed.

In <u>Ways</u> <u>to</u> <u>Writing</u>, we have suggested that peers and the instructor intervene informally at the early prewriting stages with suggestions for revision and more formally at the rough and final draft stages in response to the Audience Response Guide. You may also want to devise a three-draft stage (see Lynch and Huff below) in which students' earliest efforts to pin down the variables of the task are offered to a reader for response, the stage that Huff calls the "zero" draft. Or, you may allow students to revise a second time after you have formally evaluated the essay; this third draft is particularly useful for matters of style when, for example, sentences need combining.

Also, in using <u>Ways</u> <u>to</u> <u>Writing</u> in class, we have discovered that students often find useful comments to make about the final draft in each chapter; you may wish to ask students to write a third draft of this student work. While this exercise frustrates some students who seek closure on the process, it also demonstrates the tentativeness of writing, the truth that no piece of writing is ever perfect.

Should a three-draft process be used, you might ask students to provide self-or peer-feedback with the earlier draft, peer and teacher feedback for the middle draft, and teacher feedback for the final.

<u>What</u> <u>to</u> <u>Revise</u>

The Audience Response Guide that we have included in <u>Ways</u> <u>to</u> <u>Writing</u> is geared to questions of meaning, soliciting responses from the student reader from four points of view: as an objective reader ("What do you think the writer wants to say in this paper?"), as the reader for whom the essay was intended ("How does the paper affect the reader for whom it was intended?"), as supportive reader ("How effective has the writer been?"), and as critical reader ("How should the paper be revised?").

In answering the questions of the Audience Response Guide, students should be responding to the following sub-questions:

1. What led you to believe this was the writer's intent? Has the writer clearly announced his or her meaning? Does the paper have a shaping idea? How well is it expressed? Do the examples and evidence develop the shaping idea fully and consistently? Is the writer's voice and tone consistent with the stated meaning?

2. In answering the second question, students should refer to the questions of the Audience Analysis Guide in each chapter. Using the frame of reference the writer has prepared for his or her audience, each reader should role-

play the intended audience in responding to this question.

3. This question asks the evaluator to comment on the successes the student has had in writing the essay. Essentially, the evaluator should ask "What has the writer done well in achieving his or her goal?"

4. This last question asks "How much further must the writer go in order to accomplish her or his goal?" As students become familiar with the techniques of revision (see How to Revise below), they should make specific suggestions as to how the writer can work further to accomplish his or her intended goal.

We have suggested through the Audience Analysis Guide that the evaluation at the rough draft stage be in the form of comments on meaning that can lead to revision. Comments that require editing will not be useful at this stage since meaning is what students should be searching to express. Also, since in revising, students will be adding, deleting, and making other substantive changes, the particular passages in a rough piece of writing that require editing may not appear in the final form.

How to Revise

While student writers receive useful advice from their peers, they do not always follow it, often because they do not know how to revise. In Ways to Writing we have suggested six revising strategies first schematized in Faigley and Witte's "Analyzing Revision" (College Composition and Communication, December 1981). These strategies are adding, cutting, substituting, distributing, consolidating, and rearranging. The revisions the students have made in their essays in each chapter demonstrate how these strategies might work. Encouraging students to familiarize themselves with both the concepts and the terms and to utilize them in their peer evaluations will reinforce their learning and encourage their use of these strategies.

Showing the students how you revised the successive drafts of a writing project will not only show them why a writer revises (to clarify and develop meaning) but how revision is accomplished. Showing them how various members of the class made successful changes will also clarify the uses of the six revision strategies.

Since no two writers revise in exactly the same way, however, students should become aware of their own revision patterns. Mimi Schwartz in "Revision Profiles: Patterns and Implication" (College English, October 1983: see below) outlines nine types of revisers and suggests methods of revision that will help each one. In making suggestions for revision, the instructor may need to send the student back to the task to rethink the entire project. Rethinking an entire text may call for more skill than simply reworking one's materials for consistency or clarity. In some extreme cases, the text may have to be scrapped entirely. Helping to see the task in a new light, a re-seeing as Ann Berthoff terms it (see bibliography below), may be accomplished through asking the student questions that seek to elicit a more appropriate written response.

Evaluating Writing

At the Drafting Stage. In Ways to Writing, we have suggested a two-stage, multi-feedback evaluation process in which, for both the rough and final drafts, students receive feedback--from their "other self," their peers, and/or their instructor.

We think it important that the instructor intervene at the rough draft stage in order to provide a role model of the astute reader, one who knows how to remold a text to best convey meaning. We have suggested above that your commenting on the rough draft need not be as time-consuming as it might first appear to be. While you will need to read the students' rough drafts, you can give comments orally in conference or write them in the margins or in response to the questions of the Audience Analysis Guide. We suggest that you consult the peer evaluations and seek to comment on and complement them whenever possible in order that the writer have a coherent--even if occasionally contradictory--set of revision instructions with which to work.

Even if the student is a weak writer, you might want to suggest revisions that would make the paper the best that it can be. If you do not indicate the full scope of revision required, you may not challenge the student sufficiently or you may doom yourself to having to confront an angry student who has made the suggested revisions but not received the anticipated grade.

The tasks in Ways to Writing lend themselves to specific criteria for the evaluation of student writing, and we suggest these criteria generally in the Evaluation Scale below as well as specifically in the Revising section of the Notes on each chapter.

Final draft. Grading is, of course, a thorny issue. While students can become discouraged because of the grades they receive on their writing, they also worry when they do not receive one. We do not have a solution that will please everyone, but Ways to Writing lends itself to the following approach: since the tasks are so well defined and the various elements so carefully delineated, we have worked out in the Notes for each chapter those features that we consider

primary in fulfilling the assignment and those we consider
secondary; the following Evaluation Scale can then be
tailored to the individual task.

EVALUATION SCALE

<u>A</u>   The essay provides a well-organized response to the task
and is written with the intended audience in mind.
     A sense of pattern of development is present from
beginning to end.
     The writer supports the shaping idea and the
generalizations in the paragraphs with sufficient details or
examples. Effective transitions are used within and between
paragraphs.
     The vocabulary is well suited to the writer's task and
audience.
     Sentences reflect a command of syntax and are varied in
length and structure.
     Grammar, punctuation, and spelling are almost always
correct.

<u>B</u>   The essay provides an organized response to the task and
generally keeps the intended audience in mind.
     The writer supports generalizations and usually includes
transitions within and between paragraphs.
     The vocabulary is appropriate for the task and most of
the time avoids oversimplification or distortion.
     Sentences generally are correct grammatically, although
some errors may be present when sentence structure is
particularly complex.
     With few exceptions, grammar, punctuation, and spelling
are correct.

<u>C</u>   The essay shows a basic understanding of how to organize
this task, although there may be occasional digressions, and
the audience is not always taken into account.
     The support for generalizations is sometimes incomplete
or weak, but a basic logical structure can be discerned.
     Sentences reflect a sufficient command of standard
written English to ensure reasonable clarity of expression.
They may, however, not be sufficiently combined.
     The writer generally demonstrates through punctuation
an understanding of the boundaries of the sentence.

<u>D</u>   The essay provides a response to the task but generally
has no overall pattern of organization and does not address
the intended audience.
     Generalizations are often repeated or undeveloped,
although occasionally a paragraph within the essay does have

some structure.

Transitions between and within paragraphs may be missing.

The language is informal and the vocabulary limited.

Syntax is rudimentary and lacking in variety. Sentence structure is simple, and sentences need combining.

There may be frequent errors in sentence punctuation and in other grammatical structures.

F   The essay does not develop a response to the task. The audience is not addressed.

Generalizations are repeated or presented randomly or both. Little if any support is provided.

Language is informal, words are misused, and vocabulary is limited.

Syntax is often tangled and expression is unclear.

Errors in grammar, punctuation, and spelling occur often.

One way to deal with error, we have found, is to allow students whose texts are error-laden to revise yet another time. A method for accomplishing a meaningful third draft after the second has been marked is to group as many errors as possible under the symbol "comb" for the lack of sentence-combining and ask students to search their sentences for faulty end punctuation, lack of transition, choppy rhythm, illogical combinations, or sameness of structure. In this way, the error is not specifically noted, but at the same time students have finite choices for correction.

Although we have not included the writing process in the Evaluation Scale above, you may want to evaluate some or all features of a student's process in determining the grade for each task. For example, you may want to emphasize the value of revision by evaluating the extent to which students utilize suggestions for revision or you may want to evaluate their methodology in generating ideas. If students keep all their written work in folders, you can collect all of their materials along with the final version of their essay for easy evaluation.

We have provided in the inside cover a list of correction symbols. We know that as a labor-saving device these symbols are widely used in the profession, but we would suggest that along with the use of these symbols, teachers also offer several comments on meaning. If adding more than one comment is simply not possible, you might discuss your students' folders with them in conference two or three times during the semester.

Final Grade. In determining your students' course

grade, in addition to their process through each task, you
might want to consider their group work and their work in
their journals.

Conferring with Students

As we have indicated above, the conference can be used
to offer suggestions for revision at the rough draft stage
and to discuss a final effort once it has been evaluated.
While it is difficult to see all students in a class during
office hours, a natural sorting process will take place with
those students interested in their writing appearing on your
door step and the weaker students requesting the additional
help. You may also want to use the conference to discuss
students' journals and their passage through the writing
process.

Focusing on Form and Style

The Focus section in each chapter, located between the
sections on Writing the Essay and Rewriting, deals with
matters of form and style. Each Focus section offers a
discussion of its respective topic, followed by exercises to
reinforce its lessons and apply them to the chapter's writing
task.

In Chapter 2, the Focus section is intended to help the
student better understand what constitutes an effective
thesis statement or, as we call it, shaping idea and how to
incorporate the thesis into an effective introduction. In
Chapters 3, and 4, the Focus sections offer lessons in how to
improve transitions, how to structure paragraphs around a
topic sentence, and how to use coordination and subordination
to develop paragraphs effectively, and how to write an
effective conclusion.

The focus sections in Chapters 5, 6 and 7 deal with sentence
structure: in 5, students are introduced to sentence combining as
a way to create more complex sentences and to improve punctuation
and transitions; in 6 and 7, they learn such matters of style as
how to eliminate deadwood and how to structure more concrete, more
abstract, and more eloquent sentences. In Chapter 8,
students are introduced to ways in which connotation,
figurative language, repetition, and other such devices can
appeal to a reader's emotions. In Chapter 9, the focus is on
how different public discourse communities share different
conventions of language and voice.

In Chapter 10, the research chapter, the Focus section
introduces documentation techniques: the MLA and APA "Works

Cited" methods of citation are treated along with the more traditional method employing footnotes and bibliography. Finally, in Chapter 11, the Focus section introduces students to elements of form and style in fiction.

How to Use the Focus Sections. If you decide to utilize the integrated approach of Ways to Writing, you may choose to introduce the Focus sections chapter by chapter. Each section is situated so that the student comes upon it after completing a rough draft of an essay. The Focus section introduces material that the student then can apply immediately to revising his or her draft, and we refer back to the Focus section in the Rewriting section of each chapter.

Because it is unlikely that a class will do all eleven writing tasks in a single semester, however, you may decide to assign two Focus sections together on occasion. For example, if students are working on the task for Chapter 3 and if you are not planning to assign the task for Chapter 4, since both Focus sections deal with effective paragraphing, you might ask the students to work on the Focus sections in both chapters simultaneously (See the sample syllabi below for more about how to combine Focus sections).

We suggest that the instructor who chooses to cover one or two Focus sections per essay assignment consider making a student's application of the focus material in his or her revision a factor in determining the essay's grade. Thus, for example, before they begin their revision of the essay for Chapter 5, students might be told that a certain percentage of their grade on the essay will depend on their punctuation and transitions through the techniques of sentence combining. (See the above section on Evaluating Writing for more on grading.)

If you prefer to deemphasize the integrated approach, rearranging the sections of chapters to suit your own approach to teaching of composition, perhaps applying the material on rhetoric from one or more chapters to an assignment of your own devising, you may combine and utilize Focus sections in a variety of ways. A block of class time might be spent, for example, working on effective paragraphing, in which case students might be assigned the Focus sections in Chapters 2-4 together, just as they might be assigned more than one chapter's section on Generating Ideas or on Audience out of the integrative context of a single chapter's task, by an instructor who feels more comfortable with this sort of "block" approach. Or, particular Focus sections might be assigned to individual students who require more work on structure and style; the material then can be discussed with the student in conference.

Assigning the Handbook

Content. The Handbook included at the end of Ways to Writing is intended to serve as a reference source. It treats matters of grammar, punctuation, and mechanics traditionally, if briefly.

The first four sections of the material on grammar offer definitions and examples of the parts of speech, the parts of the sentence, and different types of sentence structure. A student may refer to these sections in order to clarify the meaning of traditional grammatical terms when they appear in a comment on the paper, in class discussion, or in a latter part of the Handbook. A complete table of contents is included at the start of the Handbook for easy reference. A commonly-used correction symbol marks each entry both in the table of contents and in the Handbook itself.

Two other sections on grammar follow, one of which offers definitions and examples of awkward sentence structure, the other of which offers definitions and examples of common grammatical errors. Included are explanations by example of how to correct such errors. The material that follows on punctuation and mechanics is organized in a similar way.

Summary exercises are included following each section.

A list of correction symbols, correlated to the entries in the Handbook, is printed on the inside back cover of the text.

How to Use the Handbook. You may refer students to the Handbook simply by utilizing the list of correction symbols on the inside back cover and announcing in class that the page numbers listed there refer to entries in the Handbook. If there is a problem in grammar, punctuation, or mechanics that seems widespread throughout the class, you may ask the entire class to look at the appropriate section in the Handbook, then review the problem in class.

The material in the Handbook on forming compound and complex sentences and on punctuation may also be used in conjunction with the lessons on sentence combining in the Focus section of Chapter 5. Similarly, the material on awkward sentence structures may be assigned while students are working on the Focus sections on style in Chapter 6 and 7.

    While the Handbook offers what we feel is a fairly
complete review of English grammar, punctuation, and
mechanics, it is, of necessity, brief. It offers only a few
examples of each matter covered, and there are only summary
exercises. It is not intended to substitute for a standard book-
length grammar.

ANNOTATED BIBLIOGRAPHY

These are sources that we used, directly or indirectly, in developing the theory and process in Ways to Writing. We have updated the bibliography for the third edition.

Theory

Booth, Wayne C. "The Rhetorical Stance." College
     Composition and Communication 14 (October 1963):139-45.
The writer argues that rhetoric be taught in Freshman
Composition. His "rhetorical stance" is based on a proper
balance between subject, audience and voice. He claims it is
a "perversion" to emphasize any one of the three.

Britton, James, et al. The Development of Writing Abilities
     11-18. London Macmillan Education Ltd., 1978.
The writers argue that the traditional taxonomy of writing
(description, narration, exposition, argumentation) is weak;
it is a description of how people should write, not of how
they do. The authors substitute a multi-dimensional model
based on function and audience: transactional, expressive,
and poetic. They stress that "expressive writing may be at
any stage the kind of writing best adapted to exploration and
discovery." The focus of the book is on the functions and
audiences of each type of writing in the model.

Connors, Robert J. "Personal Writing Assignments." College
     Composition and Communication 38 (May 1987): 166-183.
The writer traces the history of the debate between those who
would assign personal writing and those who would choose
impersonal assignments. The author argues for a middle
ground because, he says, adolescents do not know enough to
write impersonally.

D'Angelo, Frank. "The Search for Intelligible Structure in
     the Teaching of Composition." College Composition and
     Communication 27 (May 1976):142-147.
The writer issues a call for "articulate structure in the
teaching of composition" in order to devise meaningful
curricula. He distinguishes between principles of discourse
(mechanical, linguistic, and rhetorical) and forms of
discourse (traditional modes of description, narration,
exposition and persuasion or the modern modes suggested by
Kinneavy of expressive, referential, persuasive, and
literary). All should be informed by invention, arrangement,
and style.

Emig, Janet. "Writing as a Mode of Learning." College
     Composition and Communication 28 (May 1977):122-128.
This is the by now classic essay that signals the "cluster of
attributes" that writing as process-and-product possesses
that "correspond uniquely to certain powerful learning
strategies." Writing is "originating and creating a unique
verbal construct that is graphically recorded" whereas other
languaging processes utilize only two of the three criteria.

Flower, Linda and John R. Hayes. "A Cognitive Process Theory
     of Writing." College Composition and Communication 32
     (December 1981):365-387.
The authors claim that the writing process is not indiscrete
linear steps but is rather recursive. This cognitive process
model includes 1) an analysis of the rhetorical problem,
2) the constraints of the written text as it evolves,
3) plans stored in long-term memory, 4) planning,
5) translating, 6) reviewing, and 7) monitoring. The writer
moves through this process by determining goals and solving
the problems posed by these goals.

Kinneavy, James L. "The Basic Aims of Discourse." College
     Composition and Communication 20 (December 1969):297-
     304.
Kinneavy asserts that the traditional focus on exposition as
the aim of discourse is too simple and that composition
courses should embrace all aims. His schemata of the various
aims echoes Roman Jakobson's and Karl Buhler's in
distinguishing aims "by the focus on the component of the
communication process which is stressed in a given
discourse." He presents the communication process and the
corresponding aims that dominate discourse as writer
(expressive), reader (persuasive), subject (referential), and
text (literary).

Young, Richard E. and Alton L. Becker. "Toward a Modern
     Theory of Rhetoric: A Tagmemic Contribution." Harvard
     Educational Review 35 (Fall 1965):450-468.
The authors analyze four major problems of classical
rhetoric for our time: classical invention stresses the
authoritative confirmation of beliefs, discusses arrangement
only in terms of persuasion, divorces form from content, and
sees style as an external embellishment. The authors claim
that "tagmemic discovery procedures can provide a heuristic
comparable to the Aristotelian system of invention," an
epistemologic heuristic rather than an authoritarian one.

Task-Centered Approach

Donovan, Timothy R. "Seeing Students as Writers."
     Composition and Teaching 1 (November 1978):13-16.
The author believes we are settling for less than we need to
when we "treat students as students instead of writers."
Writing shouldn't be telling what the writer knows but a
pursuit of what he or she doesn't know. A writing assignment
should be based on problems for which there is no one answer
or solution.

Francoz, M. J. "The Logic of Question and Answer: Writing as
     Inquiry." College English 41 (November 1979):336-341.
The author reports on an informal experiment with a class in
which he encouraged his students to ask questions
representing a problem whose resulting dialogue of questions
and answers led to the students moving toward an independence
based on their development of the inquiry process.

Harrington, David V. "Encouraging Honest Inquiry in Student
     Writing." College Composition and Communication 30 (May
     1979):182-186.
The author poses as a problem students' inability to make use
of the best procedures for "honest" or complete inquiry. In
solving the problem, students need first to recognize a
problem worthy of inquiry. Richard Young, following John
Dewey, suggests "that the source of a problem lies in a clash
of some sort contributing to an uneasy feeling in one's
personal reaction to a situation."

Hillocks, George, Jr. "Inquiry and the Composing Process:
     Theory and Research." College English 44 (November
     1982):659-673.
The author presents the results of a study that "strongly
suggest that involving students in using the strategies of
inquiry requisite to and underlying particular writing tasks
is likely to result in far greater gains than does involving
them only in the study of appropriate models." He advocates
the "environmental" instructors (as opposed to
"nondirectional" or "presentational") who "select and organize
materials and activities which can engage students in the
processes which are important to prewriting, writing, and
editing."

Lauer, Janice M. "Writing as Inquiry: Some Questions for
     Teachers." College Composition and Communication 33
     (February 1982):89-93.
Lauer poses several questions for writing instructors: What
inner conditions are conducive to insight? "How can we
encourage students to become sensitive to the enigmas in

their experiences?" How can we teach them to "state unknowns well"? What heuristics do we teach? How can we teach them the importance of incubation? How do we do all this in the face of a culture that values common sense and doesn't want its positions threatened?

Moffett, James and Betty Jane Wagner. <u>Student-Centered</u>
    <u>Language</u> <u>Arts</u> <u>and</u> <u>Reading,</u> K-13. Boston: Houghton
    Mifflin, 1976.
Moffett and Wagner suggest nine discourse objectives for
their curriculum, and we use three of them in framing the
tasks for this book: "true stories (autobiography, memoir,
biography, reportage, journals, and so on);" information
(generalized fact); and ideas (generalized thought). The
tasks for Chs. 2-3 are "true stories;" those for Chs. 4-6
give information; and 7-11 may be considered to be
generalized thought. In some of the specific assignments
that Moffett and Wagner suggest are the roots for our tasks
in Chs. 3-5.

Tedlock, David. "The Case Approach to Composition." <u>College</u>
    <u>Composition</u> <u>and</u> <u>Communication</u> 32 (October 1981);253-261.
The author claims that "when used most effectively, the case
approach makes the need to write seem real, emphasizes
problem-solving and the writing process, and provides
students with a clear sense of audience."

Invention

Burke, Kenneth, "The Five Key Terms of Dramatism." A
    <u>Grammar</u> <u>of</u> <u>Motives.</u> Berkeley and Los Angeles:
    University of California Press, 1969, pp. xv-xviii.
Burke's pentad of actor, act, agency, scene, and purpose has
provided one of the most well-known and well-used sets of
topics for discovery. The pentad generally corresponds to
the more simply conceived journalist's questions. Burke
suggests the real complexity of these topics by pointing out
that at the points where the terms merge are "strategic spots
at which ambiguities necessarily occur."

Elbow, Peter. <u>Writing</u> <u>Without</u> <u>Teachers.</u> London and New
    York: Oxford University Press, 1973.
Still the best explanation of free writing--its processes and
purposes. "This may seem a wasteful method. You usually
throw away more than you keep. But for many people, it is
really a quicker, <u>easier</u> way to produce a <u>better</u> short piece
of writing."

Hilgers, Thomas Lee. "Training College Composition Students
    in the Use of Freewriting and Problem-Solving Heuristics

for Rhetorical Invention." Research in the Teaching of
English 14 (December 1980):293-307.
The purpose of Hilgers' study was to examine the effects on
student writing and attitudes of free writing and
"communications awareness and problem-solving" (CAPS)
heuristics. The results suggest that free writing produces
more effective results than CAPS.

Kaufer, David S. and Christine M. Neuwirth. "Integrating
Formal Logic and New Rhetoric: A Four-Stage Heuristic."
College English 45 (April 1983):380-389.
The authors believe that "formal logic has more to contribute
to argumentation than recent theory and pedagogy would like
us to believe." While formal logic both underspecifies and
overspecifies what needs to be known, a strong argument
depends upon it. They propose a four-stage heuristic:
constructing a logically sound argument summarizing the main
points in a professional essay; reevaluating the summary in
more detail to determine the writer's interpretive
background; weighing the merits of the various interpretive
frameworks underlying one side or the other; and making a
case for the higher priority of one over the other.

Larson, Richard. "Discovery Through Questioning: A Plan for
Teaching Rhetorical Invention." 19 College English
(November 1968).
Larson proposes that students come to a thorough knowledge of
their "experiences, concepts, and propositions through a
process of systematic questioning." He groups questions
according to seven types of writing assignments.

Wallace, Karl R. "Topoi and the Problem of Invention." QJS
58 (December 1972):387-95.
The author searches for modern topoi: a rhetorical evoking
of recall and inquiry for purposes of communication. He
distinguishes between topoi of subject; of audience, and of
speaker and argues for two kinds, one that helps learners
systematize what they learn, the other that provokes search
and inquiry into what may be said.

Winterowd, W. Ross The Contemporary Writer. New York:
Harcourt Brace Jovanovich, Inc., 1975.
This rhetoric text presents several approaches to invention
including a simplification of Young, Becker, and Pike's
tagmemic heuristic from their original nine-cell matrix to
the five that we have used in Ways to Writing.

Yarnoff, Charles. "Contemporary Theories of Invention in the
Rhetorical Tradition." College English 41 (January
1980):552-560.

The author discusses the systems of invention of D. Gordon Rohman, Frank D'Angelo, and Young, Becker, and Pike because "they communicate a set of assumptions inimical to students' interest." Rohman's meditation approach is too lacking in self-criticism; D'Angelo's classical topoi stress a 'fill-in the pattern' approach; and whereas Young, Becker, and Pike's tagmemic heuristic encourages critical thinking, like the others it separates ideas from their social context.

Young, Richard E., Alton L. Becker, and Kenneth L. Pike. Rhetoric: Discovery and Change. New York: Harcourt, Brace & World, 1970.
The authors present a new rhetoric and a new heuristic based on tagmemics. The information we seek about the world is based on the contrastive features of a subject (the features that identify it), its range of variation (how it can change and remain itself), and its distribution in space, time, and context. In searching for a systematic and efficient process of inquiry, the authors present a nine-cell matrix in which contrast, variation, and distribution of a subject are broken up into three additional viewpoints: particle (the static thing), wave (the dynamic thing), and field (the thing as a system or part of a system.) See Chapter 4 for a discussion of the Explorer's Questions.

Audience

Berkenkotter, Carole. "Understanding a Writer's Awareness of Audience." College Composition and Communication 32 (December 1981):388-399.
The author presents three approaches to avoiding writing to the teacher--the case approach, the audience-based heuristic of Pfister and Petrick, and Elbow's transactional--as a "healthy sign" that "we are translating our knowledge of how writers represent their audience into practical advice for composition teachers."

Ede, Lisa S. "On Audience and Composition." College Composition and Communication 30 (October 1979):291-295.
The author claims that "audience analysis is not a checklist only but is determined by the needs of the speaker as he makes decisions concerning content and desired effect of message." Students should be encouraged to formulate and analyze a rhetorical situation in order to know how to communicate successfully.

Ede, Lisa. "Audience: An Introduction to Research." College Composition and Communication 32 (May 1984):140-154.
Ede presents the research on both sides of the debate about the significance of audience awareness and analysis for the writer.

123

She calls for "an awareness of, if not involvement with, both empirical and theoretical research into a range of disciplines" by the teacher who would have a sophisticated, productive understanding of audience.

Ede, Lisa and Andrea Lunsford. "Audience Addressed/Audience
    Invoked: The Role of Audience in Composition Theory and
    Pedagogy." College Composition and Communication 35
    (May 1984):155-171.
The writers seek to illustrate that the debate over the importance of the audience to a writer oversimplifies "the act of making meaning through written discourse." The Audience Addressed model "panders to the crowd" at its extremes and ignores the writer's responsibility to the subject; it raised ethical questions. However, the constraints on the writer and the potential sources of and possibilities for the reader's role are both more complex and diverse" than are suggested by Ong and others who claim that the writer evokes the reader. The alternative is that the writer, "guided by a sense of purpose and by the particularities of a specific rhetorical situation, establishes the range of potential roles an audience may play."

Elbow, Peter. "Closing My Eyes As I Speak: An Argument for
    Ignoring Audience." College Composition and
    Communication 49 (January 1987):50-69.
As the audience may be inhibiting, the writer should write first, then think about the reader. "Writer-based" prose is often better than "reader-based" writing. Elbow quotes Vygotsky who calls our attention to the need to move from the social to the individual in our thinking and writing. The writer must also, of course, write in social situations, but it is important for the teacher to be sympathetic to personal writing.

Elbow, Peter. Writing with Power. New York: Oxford
    University Press, 1981.
The author claims that the audience both helps and hinders the writer. An actual audience is usually easier and safer to write for than the audience in the head which may be "dangerous." He suggests writers write first for friends (safe); then for an actual, even dangerous, audience; and finally for the self by now embodying the support obtained from friends.

Kroll, Barry M. "Cognitive Egocentrism and the Problem of
    Audience Awareness in Written Discourse." Research in
    the Teaching of English 12 (October 1978):269-281.
Kroll's study of the writing processes of fourth-graders

shows that writers who are egocentric do not display audience
awareness; those who can decenter their perspective do
display audience awareness. The author asserts that the
"crucial factors in an investigation of audience awareness
are not the salient characteristics of the audience but the
constructive processes operative in the mind of the writer.
We need research efforts aims at identifying the specific
cognitive correlates of audience awareness."

Kroll, Barry. "Writing for Readers: Three Perspectives on
     Audience." College Composition and Communication 35
     (May 1984):172-185.
The author's aim is to examine three views of audience that
are influential in the field: rhetorical, which as in
oratory, addresses a specific audience with the intent to
persuade; informational, which attempts to provide
information in as accessible or readable a form as possible;
and the social perspective which seeks to decenter the writer
from egocentrism to group reactions. Kroll finds drawbacks
to each: the rhetorical perceives of all communication as
persuasive, assumes the writer can learn about the audience,
and oversimplifies generally the view of the communication
process. The informational view assumes that the reader is
impoverished rather than seeing reading as an act of personal
interpretation, evaluation, and response. The social view is
vague and unhelpful since college student writers are not
sufficiently aware of others as it is and because most
writers create their own audiences based on a sense of genre
and convention. Kroll asks for a pedagogical balance among
the three.

Long, Russell C. "Writer-Audience Relationships: Analysis
     or Invention." College Composition and Communication 31
     (May 1980):221-226.
Long determines that the "writer should be a creator, not a
detective" looking for his audience. He believes that
audience analysis leads to stereotyping and inaccuracy
whereas the writer should instead encourage attitudes, ideas,
and actions in the reader.

Minot, Walter. "Response to Russell C. Long, 'Writer-
     Audience Relationships: Analysis or Invention'."
     College Composition and Communication 32 (October
     1981):335-337.
Minot does not believe that analysis and invention of
audience are mutually exclusive: 1) sociologists provide for
constructive stereotyping and 2) while the creation of an
audience is suitable for fiction, it has to be plausible
within the rhetorical situation. "In sum, writers who are
concerned about audience must both analyze and invent

audience and, in doing so, they must make generalizations about audiences."

Mitchell, Ruth and Mary Taylor. "The Integrating
    Perspective: An Audience-Response Model for Writing."
    College English 41 (November 1971):247-271.
The authors believe that the audience both judges and
motivates writing. There are three writing models: that
which stresses sincerity, that which emphasizes product, and
the audience model. English teachers are wedded to the first
two, but the authors "repudiate the ambition of English
departments to monopolize the standard-setting." The demands
of other disciplines and the marketplace should be heard.

Ong, Walter J. "The Writer's Audience is Always a Fiction."
    Publication of the Modern Language Association 90
    (January 1975):9-21.
Ong, in the most influential statement of the audience-
invoked argument, declares that speakers have audiences, but
writers have readers whom they themselves create. The
reader, then, must play the role in which the writer has cast
him.

Park, Douglas B. "Analyzing Audiences." College Composition
    and Communication 37 (December 1986):478-488.
Although the writer does need to know the identity of the
audience and how it views the subject and the writer's
intentions, traditional audience analysis is too limited.
Often the writer is dealing with a situation that brings the
audience into being: writing for a publication, for example.
Teachers should have students role-play a writer writing for
a defined audience--a journalist, a columnist, for example--
in order to analyze how the situation defines the audience.

Park, Douglas B. "The Meanings of 'Audience'." College
    English 44 (March 1982):247-257.
Park says that "powerful as the idea of audience is, it may
block thought to the extent that it presents a unified,
single, locatable something that, in fact, involves many
different contexts dispersed throughout a text." While in
highly structured situations, writers consciously focus on
audience, more often "they rely upon partly conscious, partly
intuitive knowledge of common strategies for shaping
contexts."

Pfister, Fred R. and Joanne F. Petrick. "A Heuristic Model
    for Creating a Writer's Audience." College Composition
    and Communication 31 (May 1980):213-220.
While the authors agree that a writer's audience is always a
fiction, students must nevertheless construct as near a

replica as they can of the readers who actually exist. The
authors' heuristic consists of 1) the audience's environment,
2) the audience's view of the subject, 3) the relationship
of the audience and the reader, and 4) a pre-determined
response of the audience to matters of form.

Reading and Writing

Burkland, Jill N. and Bruce T. Petersen. "An Integrative
    Approach to Research: Theory and Practice." In
    Convergences: Transactions in Reading and Writing. Ed.
    Bruce T. Petersen. NCTE, 1986.
Students need to write in a context. Research provides the
context but it is only valuable when students want to know.
Research must therefore draw on students' experiences as well
as supplying new information, draw on reader response theory,
in other words. "The process of composition and the process
of reading are based on a matrix that composes meaning as we
read, write, and interpret." The process of research
includes dialogue journals based on reading, peer reactions
to the journals, formulation of a research question, the
writing of a draft, forming of a thesis, writing of the
paper.

Hairston, Maxine. "Using Nonfiction Literature in the
    Composition Classroom." In Convergences: Transactions
    in Reading and Writing. Ed. Bruce T. Petersen. NCTE,
    1986.
Hairston offers four suggestions for using essay models in
teaching the writing process: "read rhetorically" by
analyzing the rhetorical situation the writer was confronted
with; simulate the mental and emotional process the writer
moved through; utilize your own professional writing to teach
the process; construct a "file" of essays to illustrate
strategies for revision (this latter strategy based on Paul
Escholz's "The Prose Models Approach: Using Products in the
Process," Eight Approaches to Teaching Composition) to show
how professionals support their generalizations.

Sternglass, Marilyn S. "Writing Based on Reading." In
    Convergences: Transactions in Reading and Writing. Ed.
    Bruce T. Petersen. NCTE, 1986.
When using reading as a primary source for writing, students
should construct a "frame of knowledge" for the reader: what
the reader knows and doesn't know about the subject and what
the reader's experience is with the text.

Tierney, Robert J. and Margie Leys. "What is the Value of
    Connecting Reading and Writing?" In Convergences:
    Transactions in Reading and Writing. Ed. Bruce T.

Petersen. NCTE, 1986.
Pedagogy for using writing and reading as mutually supportive
activities: when reading, keep a dialogue journal, write out
a process developed for understanding reading; while writing,
the writer will be influenced by the strategies and style of
writers read.

Focus Sections

Braddock, Richard. "The Frequency and Placement of Topic
    Sentences in Expository Prose." Research in the
    Teaching of English 8 (Winter 1974):287-302.
After examining paragraphs written by professional writers to
determine whether they have topic sentences, the author
concludes, "it is just not true that most expository
paragraphs have topic sentences in that sense." However, he
also claims that most of these professionally written
paragraphs would have been better had topic sentences been
included and that students should be taught to develop them.

Broadhead, Glenn J. and James A. Berlin. "Twelve Steps to
    Using Generative Sentences and Sentence Combining in the
    Composition Classroom." College Composition and
    Communication 32 (October 1981):295-307.
The authors present a method which "requires little new
technical terminology" and which both experienced and
inexperienced teachers can use. Students learn to "write
clear sentences with relatively short main clauses, to add
details and make inter- and intra-paragraph transitions . . .
and to use parallel and non-parallel structures
meaningfully." We have used their steps very successfully
in the classroom and present them in the Focus section of
Chapter 5.

Christensen, Francis. "A Generative Rhetoric of the
    Paragraph." College Composition and Communication
    (October 1965). Reprinted from Notes Toward a New
    Rhetoric. New York: Harper & Row, 1967.
The author extends the analogy often made between the
paragraph and sentence to a "precise structural analogy, not
with just any sentence, but with the cumulative sentence."
Paragraphs seldom utilize only one method of development but
combine methods. This combination is based on four
principles: all paragraphs develop by addition, the
direction of modification or movement must be seen, added
sentences are usually at a lower level of generality, and the
more sentences added, the denser the texture. Just as are
sentences, paragraphs are coordinate or subordinate. The
teacher can suggest that students generate material by adding
subordinate sentences to clarify and coordinate sentences to

emphasize or enumerate.

Daiker, Donald A., Andrew Kerek, and Max Morenberg. "Using 'Open' Sentence-Combining Exercises in the College Composition Classroom." In Sentence Combining and the Teaching of Writing. Eds. Donald A. Daiker et al. Studies in Contemporary Language #3, 160-169.
The authors assert that sentence-combining exercises need not bore students. "Closed" exercises help students practice certain constructions, but "open" exercises help them handle larger structures, even the essay. When asked to combine sentences that form an essay, students can learn thesis and organization, questions of coherence, punctuation and grammar, diction and syntax.

D'Angelo, Frank J. "The Topic Sentence Revisited." College Composition and Communication 37 (December 1986):431-441.
"The topic sentence can be a valuable rhetorical strategy because it can help writers to organize their ideas and it can help readers to follow the logical development of the writer's ideas." Without it, research shows, the reader will not recall as much or read as fast.

Eden, Rick and Ruth Mitchell. "Paragraphing for the Reader." College Composition and Communication 37 (December 1986):416-430.
The writers support a psycholinguistic approach, citing reader's expectations of a paragraph: unity, coherence, emphasis at the beginning and the end, and that initial sentences orient. Christensen, a formalist, with virtues (generative, deductive) and flaws (subordinators and coordinators may be at odds, students must know what they want to say at the outset, doesn't explain a paragraph sufficiently--needs a social or rhetorical motive). Teaching paragraphing should be flexible: the paragraph is not self-contained--if asking for a paragraph, should ask instead for an essay.

Stern, Arthur A. "When Is a Paragraph?" College Composition and Communication 27 (October 1976):253-257.
The author argues for a discourse-centered rhetoric of the paragraph against the logical or grammatical view of Alexander Bain, A. L. Becker, and Francis Christensen. "The logic and 'grammar' of a given paragraph are conditioned--sometimes powerfully--by what may be termed the psychologic and socio-logic of a particular rhetorical situation." Paragraphs achieve a variety of effects of tone, create transitions, do not necessarily begin with a topic sentence, nor are they functioning wholes. Total discourse should be

taught, a discourse determined by the whole essay rather than
by paragraphs.

Warner, Richard. "Teaching the Paragraph as a Structural
    Unit." College Composition and Communication 30 (May
    1979):152-155.
Warner presents a theory to make students' "pre-theoretical
notions of a paragraph explicit." Paragraphs have a common
topic (T) and also a common theme about that topic. Even if
the T sentence is missing, the topic must be understandable
from the context. Paragraphs should either have a topic
sentence or a very good reason for not having one. Other
sentences (L) either limit the kinds of information to be
developed or (D) develop the topic. A paragraph must include
a T sentence and various D sentences; the L sentence is
optional. Various combinations are possible of these TLD
sentences and generally support Christensen's theory that
"the more general sentences depend on the less general for
verification and that the most sophisticated topic sentence
is no stronger than the concrete facts which support it."

Revising

Berthoff, Ann E. "Recognition, Representation, and
    Revision." Basic Writing 3 (Fall/Winter 1981):19-32
The author claims that "without a substantial understanding
of composing as a dialectical process in which the what and
the how continually inform one another . . . there will be no
way for teachers to differentiate between revision and
editing, no way to teach revision not as a definite phase, a
penultimate stage, but as a dimension of composing. Revision
is indeed re-seeing and it goes on continually in the
composing process.... The pedagogical challenge is to help
students take advantage of (this) atonceness, to see it as a
resource, not the mother of dilemmas." She suggests
exercises like the dialogue notebook in which students must
both look and write in tandem, making observations and noting
them in their notebook. In revising, students should gloss
their paragraphs to resee what they mean and anticipate
sentence by sentence their meaning and how each sentence
suggests meaning is to continue. "Composing is thus the
activity of re-presenting concepts in language, of seeing
relationships."

Faigley, Lester and Stephen Witte. "Analyzing Revision."
    College Composition and Communication 32 (December
    1981):400-414.
The authors suggest six revision strategies based on a study
of the revising patterns of writers: adding, cutting,
rearranging, substituting, distributing, consolidating. See

discussions of these strategies in the revising sections of
Chapter 2-7.

Huff, Roland K. "Teaching Revision: A Model of the Drafting
    Process." College English 45 (December 1983):800-816.
The author's intent is to provide "immature writers with a
model of the drafting process that teaches them how to
construct a text in response to the evolving definition of an
increasingly rich and specifically designed rhetorical
problem." After choosing and limiting a topic and drafting a
rhetorical plan, Huff suggests students develop a three-stage
model: zero-drafting or discovery and initial realization of
the topic; problem-solving drafting or identification and
resolution of major conceptual and organizational problems;
and final drafting which incorporates the best possible
solution.

Murray, Donald M. "Teaching the Other Self: The Writer's
    First Reader." College Composition and Communication 33
    (May 1982): 140-147.
Murray says the act of writing is inseparable from that of
reading; one cannot write without reading. The reading of
others' finished work, however, is different from reading
one's own draft. One's "other self" must be an explorer, a
map-maker, must see where one is and where one intends to go.
The "other self" keeps track of what is taking place, gives
the self distance, provides an evolving context, articulates
problems and solutions of the text as it has evolved,
determines if what is going on "works," and provides
encouragement.

Schwartz, Mimi. "Revision Profiles: Patterns and
    Implications." College English 45 (October 1983):549-
    558.
In the author's study of the revisions of individual writers,
three profiles emerge: those that "produce and regenerate
language" (the overwriter and the underwriter); those that
reformulate structure (the restarter, the recopier, the
rearranger, and the remodeler); and those that reassess
content (the censor, the refiner, and the copyeditor). If
the instructor knows what category a student writer falls
into, he or she can help the student when difficulties arise
in revising.

Evaluation

Beaven, Mary H. "Individualized Goal Setting, Self-
    Evaluation, and Peer Evaluation." Evaluating Writing.
    Eds. Charles Cooper and Lee Odell. National Council of
    Teachers of English, 1977.

Beaven focuses on the student's role in describing, responding to, and evaluating writing. The teacher should first set up a climate of trust through individualized goal setting but should not be the only evaluator since the student would become too dependent on the teacher. In self-evaluation, students work with questions prepared by the teacher that guide them to evaluate their writing themselves. This type of evaluation does not require the teacher's time and also makes the student self-reliant, independent, and creative. In peer evaluation, the advantages are that students also develop interpersonal skills; peer models are also more efficacious than professional models.

Elbow, Peter. Writing Without Teachers. New York: Oxford
    University Press, 1973.
Elbow writes for adult writers who want to form groups but there are obvious applications for student peer groups as well: he discusses the advantages of reading aloud vs. handing out copies; the advantages of having a leader vs. having no leader; ways to respond--pointing to specific words or passages, summarizing, telling the writer what happened to you, showing your reactions through metaphorical expressions; and the dynamics of group response: everyone is right and wrong.

Flanigan, Michael C. and Diane S. Menendez. "Perception and
    Change: Teaching Revision." College English 42
    (November 1980):256-266.
The authors believe that "teaching the complexities of the revision process demands all three kinds of evaluation: by peers, teachers, and self--and at all stages of a text's development." They urge a revision guide be used with the following guidelines: 1) to discover intention and meaning and their effects; 2) to describe those discoveries for the writer; 3) to analyze why and how the reader is affected; 4) to evaluate the effectiveness in terms of the writer's purpose; and 5) to recommend strategies for change.

Griffin, C. W. "Theory of Responding to Student Writing: The
    State of the Art." College Composition and Communication
    33 (October 1982):296-301.
Griffin says that the outlines of a theory of responding to student writing are becoming clear in the literature. This theory is concerned with our orientations toward error, our verbal responses, and our students' reactions to our responses. The literature suggests we see error as stages in the learning process and as indications of how students learn. In verbalizing our responses, the main question is where we should focus our attention: on extrinsic or intrinsic matters, on the subject itself, or on communication. We need to understand how students

perceive our comments in order to guide them. The problem is how
to make nonrevisers into revisers.

Lamberg, Walter. "Self-provided and Peer-provided Feedback."
     College Composition and Communication 31 (February
     1980):63-69.
Feedback is "information on performance which affects
subsequent performance by influencing students' attention to
particular matters so that those matters undergo a change in
the subsequent performance." Self and peer feedback work by
focusing students' attention--not diffusing it (as the
instructor's feedback tends to do.) Checklists should be
used to clarify the assignment, guide peer-response activity.

Lynch, Denise. "Easing the Process: A Strategy for
     Evaluating Composition" College Composition and
     Communication 33 (October 1982):310-314.
Lynch says that evaluation should be provided at four stages
in the writing process: self-evaluation (a dichotomous
scale) at prewriting and rough draft stages; peer evaluation
(analytic scale) at first draft stage; and teacher evaluation
and grade (same analytic scale) at final stage. This final
evaluation should be followed through by having students
summarize the good and bad features of their writing.

Shaughnessy, Mina. Error and Expectations. New York: Oxford
     University Press, 1977.
In her by now classic work, Shaughnessy says that errors can
be powerful indicators of the kinds of problems basic writers
have and their strategies for solving them. She thus directs
pedagogy toward studying the process of error rather than
toward merely evaluating it.

Sommers, Nancy. "Responding to Student Writing." College
     Composition and Communication 33 (May 1982):148-156.
Sommers cites two reasons to comment on student writing: one
is to determine communication successes and failures, and the
second and more important is to help students incorporate the
presence of a reader as they write--to imagine a reader's
response. How do these goals work out in practice in marking
rough drafts? Sommers claims 1) the teacher's comments
usually sidetrack the student's own purposes. Stylistic
suggestions particularly do so as the student then feels that
style is more important than meaning. 2) Teachers' comments
are often not text-specific; the profession possesses a
"canon of commands." 3) A solution is seldom suggested.
Mainly, teachers' comments confuse process and product. The
profession must develop revising vocabularies that are
different from product vocabularies. "We need to sabotage
our students' conviction that the drafts they have written

are complete and coherent." Our written comments should not
be an end in themselves but a means of helping students
become better writers.

Williams, Joseph. "The Phenomenology of Error." College
     Composition and Communication 32 (May 1981):152-168.
Williams claims that "the language some (instructors) use to
condemn linguistic error seems far more intense than the
language they use to describe more consequential social
errors." There is also "great variation in our definition of
error, great variation in the perceived seriousness of
individual errors....We have to determine in some unobtrusive
way which rules of grammar the significant majority of
careful readers notice and which they do not."